DISORDERLY FIELDS

DISORDERLY FIELDS

by

John Mallon

DIADEM BOOKS

DISORDERLY FIELDS

Published by Diadem Books
Distribution coordination by Spiderwize

For information, please contact:

Diadem Books
16 Lethen View
Tullibody
ALLOA
FK10 2GE
Scotland UK

www.diadembooks.com

ISBN: 978-1-908026-45-3

To
Ted Deighton

CHAPTER ONE

ON **ARRIVING** at the office in Friday Bridge Agricultural Camp during the early evening of June the 20th 1980, a tall elderly man of a slight build shouted admonitions at a squat man wearing a trilby and raincoat: "If you haven't got enough money... you can't stay here... I'll give you until Monday... then you'll be off the camp!"

The man who had been shouting looked at me suspiciously. He half-shouted while moving towards me: "I'll have your money!"

I handed to him the price for a week's stay: twenty-nine pounds.

Subsequently a small elderly woman said in a mellow, pleasant voice, "Thank you." She then passed me a locker label and a week's supply of meal tickets.

I turned towards the doorway to see the other camper holding a set of bedding sheets. Standing just outside the doorway a moustache-wearing bald man—also holding sheets—jerked his head back.

As we walked the staff member, whom I later learned was known as Bald Alan, gave me sheets and a pillow case. While we passed army billets without conversing, young men spoke to me in tongues strange to my ears.

Soon after entering hut A 30, which contained twelve beds and a corresponding amount of lockers, the other camper introduced himself. His name was Arnold. As we unpacked he explained why he had been shouted at: "I received a letter at my home in Lancashire this morning... to come here today. I didn't have enough to pay for a week's rent... and I didn't have enough time to go to Building Society because it's Saturday. I thought I'd come today and pay on Monday... after I've been to Building Society. I'm only here for a week's holiday."

During the following day I familiarized myself with the life on Friday Bridge Camp. I was told that the nasty man in the office was the labour officer—and was married to the camp's secretary but behaved as if he's the boss. I was also informed that he never forgot a face and had caused a lot of grief for campers over past seasons.

During Sunday evening 1 joined the forty-seven year old carpet fitter named Arnold for tea.

While eating, the labour officer entered the dining hall and quickly arrived at our table. He snarled at Arnold: "I sincerely hope you are on the road in the morning!" He then walked away in swift strides.

Before attempting to harvest strawberries I had listened to campers' accounts of strawberry picking; one of them had earned nineteen pounds for a day's work. I conceded that I should be able to earn half that.

After working from 7.30 a.m. until 3.30 p.m. at Rockcliffe's in the region of Downham Market without stopping once, I had not earned anything close to what I had anticipated.

As I ate my packed lunch on the coach, I couldn't believe how hard strawberry picking was; and even more surprising was the vast amounts of fruit that had to be picked to earn several pounds.

I continued to work at Rockcliffe's, even though my earnings weren't fruitful. I was told that the top earners were local women who could earn thirty pounds a day—at five and a half pence per pound.

I found such claims amazing... Bald Alan told me of a local man who made fifty pounds on a bumper strawberry crop in a day. One of the disheartening aspects of this work was when working on a row, a ganger from fifty feet behind shouted, "Oye, mate, you've left some... come back and pick 'em." One camper tipped a bucket of fruit on a ganger's head. A camper in his late forties was told to pick the stalks off the fruit that he had plucked: one by one he cleaned each strawberry sitting in a tent. He didn't earn much on that day.

Even though it wasn't economical for me to stay at the camp, the people there more than compensated for it.

The accommodation was all right during dry, warm weather; but during rain a puddle of water formed on the concrete floor.

Some campers found the beds ample to make love in as well as to slumber; but I felt peevish about sleeping on urine-stained mattresses.

The entertainment in the clubhouse was charged with a seasonal atmosphere.

The most dynamic stage performer was an objectionable, garrulous, sixty-seven year old camper known as Fred from Scunthorpe, who addressed male campers as "cunty". He regularly contested the twenty-five pound prize for the best stage act—singing in a gruff, tuneless voice that failed to meet the notes that were required. Once he recited a joke: after taking half an hour to tell it, no one laughed. He justified himself to the audience of a few hundred, "It's because you're all foreigners... and don't speak English... because if you could you wouldn't have laughed so much in all your life!" Often Fred won the prize, but when he didn't he justified himself by saying he was giving others a chance.

One of those that Fred claimed he gave a chance to was a thirty-nine year old Texan known as John the Yank. He both sang and played the harmonica. John was at the camp purely to enjoy its social life; he took little interest in fruit picking. He was sometimes seen sleeping in a haystack at Rockcliffe's instead of strawberry picking.

Fred's main rival was cockney Harry. Aged in his fifties, bespectacled, with a dirty laugh and a mop of grey curly hair, he attempted to sing 'On Mother Kelly's Doorstep'; part of the way through his singing he changed the lyrics: "'She's got a hole in her shoe, a hole in her arse...'" I don't know the rest!" He didn't win the prize.

Fred and Harry's rivalry wasn't confined to the clubhouse: before starting a morning's work at Rockcliffe's they swore loudly at each other.

Old Jack the ganger told Fred he'd be down the road if he continued using bad language!

Fred subsequently accused the farmer's grandson, who was doing a Sunday morning's ganging, of being born with a silver spoon in his mouth!

Although Fred was generally regarded to be an eccentric novelty, he annoyed quite a few people. Before going to work for farmer Bates he said to three elderly women in the breakfast queue, "I'm going to Master Bates!"

Fred fancied Rose—the nineteen-year-old barmaid who worked at the clubhouse. He threatened young male campers with what he would do to them if one of them got off with her.

Unbeknown to Fred, she slept in my hut with an Italian camper.

During the strawberry season a wanted criminal had been ensnared while masquerading as a camper.

Aged in his fifties, his name was Percy Ploughshed. I watched his pettifogging sort of face preach communism about the camp, not long before the police had come to collect him.

Fred from Scunthorpe boasted that it was he who first identified Ploughshed as a masquerader.

Fred gave the following account to me and members of his hut: "I knew he was a masquerader. He rustled money all night! I watched him count it. He thought I was asleep. He said his name was Ploughshed. When he worked at Rockcliffe's he said he had an idea how to make quick money. He said, 'You're a good talker... when we weigh our fruit in, you keep the farmer talking and I'll go behind him... and cosh him over the head with a lump of wood. We'll then go into the woods and share the money.'" I said no! The police found him hiding in a dyke outside the camp... and Ploughshed wasn't his name. He was a masquerader!

The door suddenly opened, revealing a new camper who carried a suitcase.

Fred shouted at him: "Are thou a masquerader?"

The new camper didn't reply. He then quickly left the hut.

Scottish Bernard who worked in the cookhouse told me that prisoners on the run from prison had sought refuge at the camp. He had worked in 1969 at the camp with an escaped murderer who was later recaptured.

I introduced myself to the new camper at the clubhouse while sitting over pints of bitter. Tom, who came from Barnsley, said, "I felt like getting in my van and driving out of the camp... after Fred asked me if I was a masquerader!"

I asked him how he got along with Fred.

He laughed. "Fred's all right. No one can sleep... He's so loud... He's the last to sleep and the first to wake... Every morning he shouts: 'Hands off your cocks and on with your socks!'"

Tom had come to Friday Bridge for the same purpose as me—he wanted a new start in life.

Tom was more disadvantaged regarding work than I was. The labour officer had taken a dislike to him.

Tom had accidently lined up for work in the women's queue.

The labour officer snapped, "What's the matter with you, laddie... have you had a sex change, or something?"

Tom, being dark haired and squat, looked sheepish while campers about him who understood English laughed.

I felt that it was humiliating... calling a man in his early forties 'laddie'.

Subsequently, Tom wasn't given any more work. He suggested to me that we went looking for employment on private farms... But we had to be careful because campers had to work for the shareholders and directors of the camp... Even if workers didn't receive employment on Friday Bridge Camp they were still disallowed from doing work for outside employers.

Soon after discreetly driving early out of the camp we found work picking strawberries on a farm at Guyhirn.

Although the rate of pay was better than at Rockcliffe's we only worked there for one day. Tom believed the farmer had paid him for less than he had picked. The farmer denied this.

On the following morning the labour officer, in long strides, quickly came up behind Tom's van; but Tom pulled away before we could be reached.

We found a job at Wales Bank. Before starting work the foreman threatened to sack us if we didn't pick the strawberries properly.

As the days of strawberry picking went by we found the foreman to be a friendly man.

The farmer was also friendly—and paid at a better rate than Rockcliffe paid.

At one time he had employed campers, but had stopped doing so.

I later heard that another local farmer wouldn't employ campers because he disliked the labour officer.

During one evening Tom looked at the work list, and not seeing his name, said out loud, "I won't be staying next week!"

At the same time the labour officer approached and commented on the remark that wasn't addressed to him: "You wouldn't get any work if you did!"

Tom said to me that he was going to live in his three-wheeler van and work for private farms. He asked me if I was interested in doing the same thing.

As much as I enjoyed the social life at the camp, I realized how hard it was trying to earn a week's board on earnings made from strawberry picking. I decided to work with Tom until the better paying crops that I had been told about had started.

Tom and I continued to pick strawberries at Wales Bank. We slept at different spots—sometimes in Wisbech, another time at Friday Bridge... all depending on how much hassle the police gave us.

Tom slept with his head against the steering wheel, whilst I slept upside down in the passenger seat.

Once the work at Wales Bank finished, we hardly had any money and found the prospect of more work difficult due to the strawberry season starting to end.

While hungry in Wisbech, a knock on the van's window awoke us one afternoon. It was Col whom I had known at the camp. I was surprised to see his hideous face looking through the passenger's window—because he was someone I disliked.

He said that a contractor asked him if we wanted to work for him picking strawberries.

We accepted.

We then took Col to his tent which was situated on the periphery of a field at the back of Friday Bridge Camp. He camped with two students named Pete and Paul. The three of them had left the camp for economical reasons.

It was a convenient area to be based: campers fetched us leftover food; Pete sneaked to the camp for a shower; and Tom hooded his head and helped himself to a flask of hot drink from the tea urn—which was put out each afternoon so that the workers could have a cup of tea after returning from work.

Due to the sparseness of the contractor's crop, work was irregular and the derived earnings were lower than those earned at Rockcliffe's. Consequently Tom and I attempted to run a taxi service from outside the entrance of Friday Bridge Camp. After managing to persuade just one passenger to travel in Tom's van we abandoned this venture.

Subsequently, we parted company with Col, Pete and Paul—and re-based ourselves at Wisbech. During this time the van's battery failed, taking away the transport we would need to travel the Fens looking for work. We didn't have enough money to buy a meal, let alone a second-hand battery.

Believing in the good old saying, 'No one starves in Britain', we went to the Social Security Department in Wisbech.

There, an official who looked to be a year from retirement, said to us, "We don't give money to gypsies!... And there's still strawberries to be picked!"

I retorted, "The strawberries have finished!"

"We've been given orders not to give money to you people," was her rejoinder.

We were subsequently given an interview with another official who looked as old as the first official.

I said to him, "I live a very long way from home"—after he suggested that we returned to our hometowns.

He added, "I cannot give you money. I can only suggest that you try at the Peterborough office... but there is a four-day waiting time."

I countered, "We've got no money... and the battery of our van is broken!"

He politely finished, saying, "There's nothing I can do."

Tom and I remained in his van for a couple of days without having anything to eat. There was no comfort in this area for people like us. So many of the pubs in this area had signs in their windows stating: 'No vandwellers.'

During a Sunday afternoon sleep I was startled due to someone knocking on my window. I watched an official looking card being forcefully shown. The same occurrence happened at Tom's side of the van.

On vacating the vehicle a tall well-dressed, fair-haired man searched the van while his dark-haired companion looked underneath the vehicle.

Tom and I looked bemusedly at one another.

The fair-haired man asked, "Will you go to the Police Station for questioning?"

We were questioned for an hour.

I was impressed by the clever construction of their questions... No threats and sarcasm were made to us... which I had previously witnessed being used by less clever law enforcers.

Their enquiries were constructed around our pauperism. Tom and I honestly answered their questions which dramatically altered in subject from question to question.

Casually the fair-haired detective asked, "Where do you go drinking?"

"The Chequers," I replied. (We hadn't been there since we had work.)

Making an expression exhibiting both admonition and triumph, he retorted, "The Chequers at Friday Bridge was robbed on Friday!"

"Much taken?" I asked.

"Cigarettes and money," he said with an insinuating smirk. He added, "You are poor, desperate and hungry!"

I returned, "Yes... but we're not poor enough to steal!"

Consequently he gave the other detective a look that said 'they are innocent'.

They subsequently checked to see if we were wanted for crimes in our home areas... Once they discovered we weren't, we were told to go.

On checking for mail at the general post office at Wisbech, Tom found that his sister-in-law had sent him money—which was sufficient in value to be able to buy an old battery.

After having a meal we both decided to see what Kent was like regarding seasonal work.

We toured areas in the vicinity of both Borough Green and Holton Kirby for seasonal work... but were told on one orchard that we could have work in a couple of weeks... The rest of the farmers said that there was nothing doing.

On the way down from Wisbech to Kent we stopped at a house in Cambridge. After knocking at the door the occupant asked what Tom wanted.

He replied, "I want some water."

The woman asked, "What for?"

"For a flask of tea."

She refused.

Incidentally, Col had knocked at a stranger's house and asked if he could have a bath. I don't know what the owners reply was to that!

We returned to Cambridgeshire to work on the blackberry season.

We had been offered work on this crop by the farmer whom we had worked for at Wales Bank.

There were many vandwellers there—where there were only several of us working on the strawberry crop.

The farmer's attitude had changed: he referred to Tom and me by our Christian names during the strawberries; while working on the blackberries, he addressed us as 'mate'.

The rate of pay was worse than what he had paid for the strawberries.

Consequently, we went to meet the contractor whom we had picked strawberries for. We met with him and Col outside his home. I asked him for work—after telling him the rate of pay we had earned.

The contractor emphatically asked, "Who is this man who paid you three pence a pound? I pay nine pence."

I returned, "He's a bloke in his early forties called Parsons."

The contractor excitedly responded, "You worked for Fiddler Parsons... That's young Fiddler... He's worse than old Fiddler!"

While we conversed Col gave an expression... indicating that he knew this man of old—but he wouldn't have been able to identify Fiddler Parsons if he fell on him!

We subsequently harvested blackberries until the season ended.

On September the 20th, I returned to Friday Bridge Camp. Due to my arrival being late in the evening, the labour officer had to be called from the club; this was done by Bald Alan.

Once inside the office the labour officer remarked, "You've been here before... I remember you by your hair."

Subsequently Bald Alan took me to a hut that accommodated a Turkish camper as well as myself.

On the following morning I met Tom. He had arrived early during the previous day. Even though the labour officer didn't like him, Tom had previously been told by veteran campers that there would be plenty of well-paid work in September.

We both picked apples at Shippey's in Newtown... finding the pay better and much easier than strawberry picking.

The work was controlled by Monty, whose large bulk made no hindrance to him quietly moving through the trees. In various parts of the orchard his vociferous voice was heard condemning workers who bruised apples—and for other things.

He sacked a Moroccan for having saliva on his chin—accusing him of sleeping while being paid on a day rate.

Two other Moroccans were fired—due to them on a piece rate picking up apples from the ground.

Sometimes when Monty had sacked campers, the labour officer didn't know. Consequently they were sometimes sent back to Shippey's.

Monty sent those campers back in the van that had brought them. One Welshman looked like a hunted animal as he stood in a circle of twenty-odd campers.

Monty said to the van driver, "Roy, take him back... I sacked him yesterday!"

I spent several weeks picking apples, mostly at Shippey's as well as harvesting pears at Ayres.

Ayres had a reputation for being a good employer—which I found to be true... A day rate was paid without the hostile threats that I had observed at Shippey's. Two old gangers at Ayres joked with campers while they supervised the work.

Tom fell from a ladder while pear picking at Ayres.

On the following morning, due to him being injured, I accompanied Tom to a doctor's at Wisbech.

Once we had returned to the camp, the labour officer marched up to us and demanded to know where we had been. He didn't believe that Tom had been to seek medical attention.

He blurted, giving us a look that said he believed we had been working privately, "I've been doing this job for twenty-six years!"

While walking away from us he inquired, "You do want to work?"

"Yes," we returned.

He added, "As long as I know."

Tom changed his mind: he and a few other campers moved to Elm, to pick apples on a private farm where a free place to live was provided.

During the season I changed to different huts. I got on well with my Turkish roommate... but the lovemaking that he performed with his Welsh girlfriend disturbed my slumber!

I shared a hut with six Moroccans; I also got on with them—but they made too much noise.

I eventually moved into a hut housing British campers.

The eldest camper was in his sixties. His name was Bill, but was known as The Undertaker. He was a lonely, sad figure clad in a trilby and raincoat. He had first arrived at the camp not long after the Second World War... to help farmers harvest their crops. This was before it had officially opened as a working holiday camp.

He seemed to enjoy waking us up early on Sunday mornings playing Indian music. This prematurely woke a bouncer named Ray, a former bank clerk called Phil, and a holidaying fireman known as Dick the Walker.

On Wednesday evenings most of the campers went to the disco at The Sportsman in Elm.

The Sportsman's publican welcomed the alcohol drinking campers, but was annoyed by the Muslims who went onto the dance floor with bottles of cold tea that they had fetched from the camp.

I met Tom there. He earned sixty-two pounds a week.

Col also went to The Sportsman. He earned ninety-two pounds a week plus free accommodation working for Farmer Willett. He earned in the region of forty pounds more than what the average camper made at Friday Bridge at that time of the season.

We finished work at Shippey's picking up windfalls.

Some of the workers consisted of staff members like Bald Alan and The Head Barman—who worked in the fields on their days off. I watched a camper called John the Cowboy, aged in his fifties, outwork much younger men as he sped over grass and dirt with back kept bent and hands working at a very fast pace. Monty watched us being paid and commented, "That should go well with your dole!"

After working for Shippey I briefly picked apples for Masons in Lincolnshire. Due to the trees not being pruned, my pay was so low that it wasn't worth getting out of bed for.

The last job I did was onion picking for the courgette company which was controlled by the Welsh gangers—who had been in charge of a part of the courgette crop; the other section was controlled by the Top Ganger.

The pay for this work was lower than for windfalls; and this graft was harder, due to layers of ice on the vegetables.

The fastest worker on the onion beds was a local woman in her seventies named Mrs March.

The Welsh gangers seemed to be well in with the boss of the courgette company. They drank with him; and he had offered them work in March planting onions.

There was a party on the official date of closure at the camp during late October.

John the Cowboy played his piano accordion, while John the Yank sounded his mouth organ.

And veteran camper P.J. who only entered the club on the last day of each season drank beer and whisky.

John Mallon

CHAPTER TWO

ON JUNE THE 6TH 1981 I returned to Friday Bridge Camp... due to the job that I had intended to do in Jersey on the potato crop having fallen through.

The labour officer silently observed me as I waited at the counter in the office.

His wife looked up from the forms on the counter. She gently spoke, "Hello John... back again for another season?"

"Yes," I returned.

After I paid for a week's board I was led to my accommodation by a swarthy complexioned biggish man.

I asked the sinister looking man, "Are you new?"

The man whom I later found out was known as Japanese John replied in a northern English accent, "No. I couldn't make it last year."

I was placed in a hut that contained English, Irish, Scottish and Welsh campers.

At this stage of the season there were about fifteen campers on the camp.

The only camper that I knew was a veteran known as John the book, who was one of three campers in employment.

19

Due to the crops not being ready the labour officer permitted campers to try and find private employers until directors and shareholders were ready to employ them.

Consequently I joined three Irishmen and an Irishwoman in seeking local work.

A staff member known as Big John enjoyed seeing campers without work. Aged in his fifties, he sneered in a Polish accent as he sat on a chair painting the outside of a hut, "The strawberries are very small!" His thumb almost touched an index finger, to demonstrate the diminutive size of the fruit.

I remembered Big John from last season.

He told me then that in 1980 he earned six pounds a day working in the cookhouse; and in 1955 he earned six pounds a day as a camper—working at Smedley's fruit factory.

After a week of searching unsuccessfully for work I decided to leave Cambridgeshire.

During early July I returned to Friday Bridge Camp.

As Japanese John led me to a hut he said, "Some campers have requested you in their hut."

Soon after entering the hut I found that it was Portuguese Jorge who had asked for me to be put in his hut. I had known him from earlier in the season. I also shared this hut with the girlfriend of Jorge: Irish Joanie—and with four Turks and four Japanese men.

The four middle-aged Welshmen had returned, in anticipation of being able to work as gangers on the courgette harvest.

On looking at the worklist, they found themselves to be employed at Ayres. After a week of strawberry picking, and earning half what they had earned as gangers, and having to work a lot harder, it was apparent that they were only earning enough to pay the thirty-one pounds a week board that was required of them.

The reason why they were sacked was that three of them—Bob, Shaun and Terry—didn't arrive in March to plant onions as they said they would.

They had justified themselves on the grounds that they would still be gangers, saying, "There's no-one else to do the job!" But they had made the same mistake as many other people had done at Friday Bridge Camp—they had overestimated their worth!

At the end of the week—with suitcases in hands and tails between legs—they returned to Ebbw Vale.

Although the work for courgette cutters had increased I found myself working on the strawberry crop and at the process factory.

On the way to Rockcliffe's Fred from Scunthorpe shouted encouragement; but most of Fred's work involved shouting! His straw-covered back at the end of the day indicated that he'd been sleeping in between rows of strawberries.

On one Sunday morning Rockcliffe employed a coachload of campers to work on a crop in which the locals had already picked, taking the big fruit... The small strawberries were left for the campers. For a morning's work wages of between fifty pence and a few pounds were earned.

No matter what the reason was for a camper not being able to pay for accommodation... they were ordered to leave the camp.

Raging threats were heard about the camp office at dawn... until the morning's workers had left the camp. These were the familiar sounds made by the labour officer; while in the office he drank rum and beer.

Fred from Scunthorpe was the only camper I knew who could get away with things he said to the labour officer.

On seeing that he was working for a Jewish employer, Fred from Scunthorpe turned from the worklist and shouted at the labour officer who conversed with a man sitting in a van, "I'm not working for no Jew!"

Once the Jewish employer had driven away, the labour officer burst into laughter.

Once the strawberry crop had finished there was a dearth of work.

I spent about three weeks unemployed.

The labour officer operated a pool system, whereby unemployed campers were in reserve for those who wouldn't or couldn't go to work; these usually weren't given work again—and often told to leave the camp.

Usually several out of a pool of about fifty campers received work.

Having seen their names listed under 'pool', some campers waited at the swimming pool! That enraged the labour officer. He sent Japanese John to bring them to their proper place. John always accompanied the labour officer at work time.

I had discovered that the reason John couldn't be on the camp in 1980 was because he had been in prison.

Some campers made beds and slept out through the night while they queued.

Sometimes there were fights in the labour pool... due to place jumping.

The unhappiest looking people I saw were a group of Polish students. I didn't see one of them smile during the three weeks they were there. Due to them not receiving work they formed picket lines... to try and stop the people who received work every day from going to the courgette fields.

During August I was allocated a day's work plum picking at Shippey's.

I watched Monty's massive shadow move through the plum trees. Subsequently, rigorously announced reprimands were given to workers on other rows.

Once the din had stopped a bespectacled man aged in his late fifties walked down my row, then said to me: "You're lucky he didn't shout at you... you've left loads behind!"

I returned, "I'm not lucky... I'm well in!"

Due to 1981 being a hot summer, considerably more campers were employed on the courgettes, including myself.

The four Welsh gangers had been replaced by Bald John, Burmese Marco, Lincoln and Moroccan Hassan.

I cut in all these gangs, which worked, with the exception of Hassan, at Laddus fen.

I found Marco's gang to be the best to work in—the jokes and humorous tales that he told helped to relieve the monotony of the work. I had known him superficially in 1980.

Bald John was an unpopular camper; and regarded himself to be fortunate to be a ganger during his first season at the camp.

During the day that I had worked with him he said that he didn't know what he had done right: whilst being with sixteen men the boss of the courgettes had said, "Hello John"… and nothing to the others!

One of the Welsh gangers who had returned to harvest other crops, named Mervin, had said to me regarding Bald John, "If he says anything to me, he'll get it in the face!"

"Even if he says good morning?" I enquired.

"Even if he says good morning!" he returned.

I was surprised to see Mervin and Shaun return after a month of them leaving the camp. Shaun returned to the courgette fields as a cutter, while Mervin refused to as a matter of principle.

Ironically, Mervin should have remained as a ganger—because he hadn't agreed to return to plant the onions in March—which Bob, Shaun and Terry had done.

Subsequently Mervin received one of the best jobs on the camp, driving a corn harvester, earning ninety-four pounds a week.

It was also Lincoln's first year. His clean appearance and English reserve gave him the air of a scoutmaster. Lincoln worked his gang much harder than the other gangers did. While the others took their gangs steadily through the rows, Lincoln rushed his workers. Even after breaks, while the other gangers, in a reluctant manner, returned to work, he ran to his knife and bucket.

Subsequently I was sent to cut courgettes at Jew House Drove, where The Top Ganger and Moroccan Hassan had gangs.

I had known The Top Ganger from 1980; he resembled a blond rock star. He indicated to me that he wanted to be my friend which seemed to be on the basis of the rough time Tom and I had known in 1980.

I really enjoyed both working and socializing with the high profile Top Ganger. He believed in having a good laugh at work.

Within the gang were laid off cookhouse workers.

One was Phil from Rotherham who said that a workmate reserved a special egg for the courgette boss. Phil laughed as he said that he deliberately gave the reserved egg to the camper queuing before the boss. Phil added that his workmate had started to panic, and said to the boss that he'd make him a special egg.

The boss said that he'd have the same as the campers. The eggs were in bits in the tray. Phil's workmate said that he didn't know that he liked eggs like that. The boss said that he didn't.

Phil also said that the courgette boss, who was in charge of the cookhouse, entered the kitchen as he dropped a pile of plates. Regarding broken plates, the courgette boss said to him: "Saves washing them!"

Phil was like Stevie, in the respect that they both worked in the cookhouse, and that, for a reason not known to me, were paid at a higher rate than the other cutters.

Stevie, who also originated from Yorkshire, said that the kitchen worker who kept a special egg for the courgette boss, had put a hand down his trousers saying, "I might as well scratch my balls... because no-one else will!" He then used the same hand to put sausages on campers' plates. His nicknames, unbeknown to him, were Hygienic Hank and Mucky-hand Mike. Although his proper name didn't resemble either of these.

The Top Ganger helped to displace the boredom by, in turns, sending in a cutter to help the tractor driver collect crates of courgettes and to help Hassan.

The tractor driver was named Gus. He had come out of retirement to do this job; and being German, he had been a prisoner of war in East Anglia. After the Second World War had ended he remained in East Anglia. I found Gus to be easy-going and quiet.

The general atmosphere on the courgette beds was hassle-free under old Joe the foreman.

Hassan's gang consisted of north and central Africans. Two of the central Africans were George and Joe; both of them were built like cruiserweight boxers. During one night they had huddled nervously in a hut—due to a woman having passed the outside of their door—they were concerned that she had seen them in their dressing gowns!

I liked the gentlemanly Christianity that they espoused through their personalities.

Very rarely did the Top Ganger's gang alter, but one of the campers that joined it when it did, was a holidaying Yorkshire miner named Big Kevin, who had been going to the camp for thirteen years.

In conversation The Top Ganger told him that he was earning beneath the legal national rate.

Big Kevin retorted, "If I'm getting one pound forty an hour... I'll make sure I do one pound twenty's worth of work!"

After several weeks working on the courgettes I found myself in the pool queue again—due to the vegetables having passed their peak.

One morning I found myself to be first in the queue, but by that time all the reserves that were needed had gone to work.

Suddenly, someone shouted, "I'll have one more!"

It was Monty; even though he had enough workers, I was fitted in.

He told me to sit on the van's floor.

Soon after we had arrived at the apple orchard in Newtown I paired off with Phil, who I worked with in The Top Ganger's gang.

Monty arrived. Then he asked me how I was. He turned to my partner—who hadn't worked at Shippey's previously—then gave him a severe telling off, threatening him with the sack if he didn't do what he was told!

A sacked camper went to the office pursuing an hour's pay.

On leaving the office the labour officer snarled after him, "And that's all you're worth!"

A punk rocker didn't know where his workplace was.

The labour officer yelled as he pointed, "Get over there! Alvin Stardust... or whatever your name is!"

The labour officer threatened a Geordie skinhead that he wouldn't be given any work.

While walking away from the work pool, the camper retorted, "I'm going to phone the press!"

"Wait. I'll find you work!" countered the labour officer.

Veterans of the fifties said that three Fleet Street typists had gone to the camp on a week's holiday then. They later published a complaint about Friday Bridge Camp in a newspaper, although I was told that the conditions then were better than those that I had known twenty-five years later.

The labour officer asked a camper where she came from.

While queuing for work, she replied, "Hamburg."

He returned, "I was there during the war ... I bombed it!"

During one morning, just after workers in the pool queue had walked from it having abandoned hope of work for that day, Bald Alan took myself, Joe of the cookhouse and Shaun of the Welsh gangers, towards his van, and whispered, "Go back to the queue... Bates wants workers!"

After a short wait, the labour officer instructed us to go on the trailer of the truck that had stopped.

Our work involved finishing apple trees that hadn't been cleaned of their fruit by vandwellers. We were paid at such a good rate that the three of us earned more in a few hours than a day's courgette cutting made.

We spent most of each day relaxing, telling stories and jokes.

Joe said that one Saturday morning he entered the kitchen to find Big John and the breakfast cook to be sleeping while the bacon was engulfed in flames.

Due to Joe waking them up, the breakfast cook said, "Piss off!"

Campers then began knocking on the other side of the hatch for their breakfasts. The breakfast cook opened the hatch… then shouted, "Piss off!"

He then went to bed—and remained there until the following Tuesday.

They later explained their behaviour to Bodna, the head cook.

Big John said that the breakfast cook had put vodka in his tea—and he hadn't realized this; while the breakfast cook said that he was unaware that Big John had added vodka to his tea!

Joe and other male members of The Top Ganger's Clique had a contest to find out which of them could seduce the most women… A gold star was awarded for each verified conquest. Joe, having accumulated twenty-four stars, won.

He said that there wasn't a woman on earth that he couldn't seduce.

Joe explained, "To get the girls... make them laugh and always tell them lies!"

While working at Bates Joe left the camp in anticipation of pursuing hotel work in Germany.

Both Shaun and I intended to work in Greece.

Soon after Joe left Shaun and I were given work on a potato harvester at Bates.

I found The Top Ganger to be the most gifted comedian that I had witnessed. His humour showed more talent than the stupid-student, Monty Python derived comedy I had observed. He entertained twenty or so of us night after night with his original funniness—at The Sportsman and in the clubhouse.

There were also marvellous entertainers who performed on stage at the club. One of them was Ritchie from Thailand. Although he was billed as a singer, his act was so funny that locals packed the clubhouse to watch and hear him.

Towards the end of the season the boss of the courgettes put on a party for people who had worked for him.

It was a surprise to have high quality food, prepared by outside caterers—which hadn't come out of a tin can.

It was also a surprise to be able to drink as much fine German wine and beer as we wanted to.

During the latter part of the season, campers and staff members spoke about employment in Greece.

A camper named Andy had worked in Greece during 1980. He tried to sell hand-drawn maps of Nafplion for five pence each. He also promised campers that he liked to find work for them there; and threatened people that he didn't like, saying they wouldn't get work there.

A local named Jacko was caught cheating by Andy while playing cards.

Andy said he wouldn't receive work in Greece.

Jacko replied, "I don't want to go to Greece."

Andy retorted, "I don't care. I'll still make sure... no-one will give you work in Nafplion!"

A person who had worked in Greece at the same time as Andy told Shaun and me to take no notice of him. He said disdainfully, "He's promising people jobs... and he couldn't find work himself!"

The most sensible information I received regarding seasonal work in Greece was from a staff member named Ken. He was a popular staff member because he had a reputation as someone who helped campers. He also had the reputation as the best apple picker on Friday Bridge Camp.

Bald Alan said that Ken had earned fifty pounds in a day picking apples.

Soon before the official end of the season, Bald John, while working on the courgettes, broke a leg.

Consequently officials from the Department of Health and Social Security visited the courgette boss, asking for compensation.

The only thing that Bald John received from the courgette boss was a lifetime ban from Friday Bridge Camp!

With reference to Bald John, The Top Ganger said, "There'll be no no marks in our gang next year!"

CHAPTER THREE

SHAUN, MERVIN AND I went to Athens by bus. During the journey Mervin's feet had badly swollen. Once in Athens two West countrymen whom we had met on the coach, named Andy and Jeff, took us to a hostel named Festos.

Soon after booking in the three of us took a walk through the Plaka, observing people, traffic and buildings during a November afternoon of 1981.

A well-dressed man in his forties asked us, "Do you want to go to a nice bar… with nice girls?"

Mervin walked towards the man… and Shaun followed them into The Ladybird bar. I went after them.

A smarmy, grinning barman called, "A beer!" as he handed three glasses of lager across the bar.

As soon as we began to drink, two women came to us. One stood by Shaun and the other was at Mervin's side.

Each woman asked, "Will you buy me a drink?"

Shaun and Mervin refused.

As I followed Shaun and Mervin to the exit, the barman snapped, "That will be one hundred drachmas each!"

We paid, then left. The three of us knew that we had been conned: a bottle of that lager, Amstel, cost fifty drachmas; a glass consisted of a third of that volume.

Mervin looked embarrassed. He said, "We would have spent more in there than that if we hadn't been ripped off!"

We continued to walk and unintentionally found the bar that was known as a meeting place for people who had worked at Friday Bridge. Just as we were about to enter the Alexander bar, someone shouted. We watched a large man running to us. It was Andy from the camp.

The four of us entered, to see Col serving drinks. I hadn't seen him for more than a year. He said that vandwellers who he had fallen out with had caused him to leave the Wisbech area.

Andy had virtually no money—hence he became charitably drunk—on us. Consequently he promised us work.

I told him that we had been conned at The Ladybird bar. He said that was where a friend of his, who had served behind the bar at Friday Bridge Camp, had worked. She asked customers for a drink, ordering the most expensive… and the barman gave her water and charged the customers for champagne!

After a few days in Athens we caught a bus to Nafplion.

We waited outside Jorgo's cafe which we had been told was the meeting place for seasonal workers. The three of us watched trucks dropping off workers into the coldish night— hoping for a recognition to be made. We first saw Gus, an English greaser, whom I had known at the camp in 1980. He told us that he had worked in a factory at Athens shovelling talcum powder since the last time we had picked apples at Shippey's together.

Subsequently, Ken jumped from a truck. After shaking hands he took us to The Acropol Hotel. I was amazed how clean and well-furnished the room that we moved into was.

Later that night Ken took us to The Four Brothers for a meal. I told Ken about us being conned in Athens.

He said that the same thing had happened to a friend of his in 1979. His friend had got drunk in a bar... and thought he was in heaven, buying beautiful women champagne. Once sober he found that virtually all his money had gone. He had to go home.

After our meals, Ken took us to The Yacht Club where we met Andy. He was so drunk and reiterated that he would find the three of us work in the morning.

Mervin and I waited for Andy outside Jorgo's cafe but he didn't arrive.

While we waited a young man offered us work. Several people entered the rear of a lorry.

The gang was led by an old, big-bearded scouser named Charlie. At meal times his penis protruded through a huge hole in his trousers—in full view of three Australasian women who sat near him.

As the days went by Shaun and Andy joined us. Andy appointed himself as an assistant ganger. He shouted orders, to no-one in particular; and kept walking back and forth counting and re-counting rows of boxes holding picked oranges.

But I saw him, peeping from behind a tree, while holding a cigarette in the hand that held the same orange, for a few minutes.

After twelve days in this gang, the most impressive orange picker that I had seen work in it—Dutch Mike— asked me to join a gang that he was starting.

Marco, who had recently arrived in town with Portuguese Jorge, joined me in Mike's gang. He and Jorge had stayed on at Friday Bridge Camp—building bird pens for the courgette boss.

I had known Marco as a courgette ganger—but he was much better picking oranges than cutting vegetables.

Dutch Mike's organization and workers were so good that we earned more money than I earned in Charlie's gang—in half the time during a working day.

The Yacht Club. Ken, second from left. Bald Alan, right.

In Charlie's gang a Spanish worker wanted water to wash his hands. Charlie refused, saying, "If you want to wash your hands, piss on them!"

After a couple of days in operation, Dutch Mike's gang disbanded due to the work finishing.

I subsequently experienced unemployment lasting for several days, until the West countrymen, Andy and Jeff, whom I had met during the coach trip from London to Athens, offered me work.

This gang was headed by a comical man from northern Greece named Visili. He spoke seven languages... When speaking English Visili used an exaggerated American accent... adding the word 'man' to the end of each sentence. Visili complained that the cost of living in Nafplion was double what he had known in his own town.

I hadn't known such vocational chaos in previous places of work as I was made aware of in Visili's gang. Visili seemed to have an illogical perception of efficiency: he took the most difficult options even though easier choices were available to him.

The most impressive workers I saw in this gang were Andy and Retsina Ray.

Andy and Jeff were lifelong friends who shared their collective earnings. While Andy picked oranges regularly, Jeff didn't work so much. While anticipating a day in an orchard, Jeff looked to the clement sky, then remarked, "It looks like another day for the beach!"

Andy said to me, "I'm really pissed off! He's drinking the money faster than I earn it!"

Jeff, at night, could be often found drinking in The Yacht Club with his Australian girlfriend, Shaun, Mervin and Bald Alan.

Soon before the Christmas period I became unemployed again—and, because of a lack of work, remained without a job for nine days.

But this didn't affect Shaun and Mervin: they had stopped working a couple of weeks before Christmas—and spent most of their time getting drunk. Both wore suit jackets— and were among the few seasonal workers to be allowed service in The Yacht Club.

Mervin gave me the impression that he considered seasonal work to be beneath him. Mervin stressed that he was a tradesman—and he didn't have to pick oranges like me because he had plenty of money; and so did Shaun. Mervin's bitterest regret was that he was forty-one years of age instead of twenty-two.

Soon after Christmas Shaun, Mervin and Bald Alan left Nafplion. I replaced Alan by sharing a room with Ken.

Early in the New Year of 1982 I went from gang to gang doing short-term employment. I worked for agents such as Mario, Costas, Vangellis—and ones whose names I didn't know.

Vangellis employed several gangs—but some of the workers didn't receive full payment. He just couldn't be located. The people, who were eventually paid, waited for a few weeks before he was prepared to pay them.

I did a day's work in a gang whose agent was Vangellis—where a partially drunk group of people began picking—but ended the day's work close to being inebriated due to so much retsina being available to us.

I told Ken about Vangellis not paying what he owed. He said that the same thing had happened to him a year earlier regarding another employer of orange pickers. Ken explained: "We were working for a factory who owed us a week's money. We all went there for our money and were told the manager was in Athens. We said we wouldn't go until we got our money. The police came and asked us what was going on, and we told them. They in turn told them if they didn't pay us... they would go to jail. They paid up!

As the days of January went by, more people from Friday Bridge Camp arrived such as Bald John, The Top Ganger and his girlfriend.

I wasn't in the only group who travelled to do seasonal work. The New Quay mob consisted of twenty-odd young people who worked at hotels in Cornwall during summer—followed by a few months of orange picking, finishing before returning to New Quay doing hotel work on Spetse.

A few days after the first week of January Marco and Portuguese Jorge got me a job in their gang, which was headed by a Lebanese man called Spero. His gang mostly consisted of Friday Bridge and New Quay people.

Ken was the most impressive picker that I had seen in this gang, while Marco's interest in orange picking became disorientated on seeing women that he fancied.

While we worked on the same tree Marco said to me, "Look at her arse!" He then ran to the tree where the Kiwi schoolteacher picked and wrestled her to the grass where they playfully frolicked!

Portuguese Jorge had come to work in Nafplion for a different reason from the rest of us: he had skipped doing national service. Hence he was unable to return to Portugal.

During the latter part of the season we changed from picking navel oranges to harvesting juice oranges.

Spero, who was stout and squeaky-voiced, allocated the hardest work to the women—picking up the fruit from the ground—and paid them less than what the men received— who also picked up from deck—and even those males who relaxed standing on ladders—dropping oranges down. The women who refused to go to bed with him were sacked.

I had wondered why so many other illegal workers had been forced to stop working due to police pressure—yet we were allowed to go to the orchards unhindered. A confidante of Spero's explained to me that our ganger was left alone because he provided information to the police regarding drug users.

An agent took advantage of us being the only gang working: after a long argument between Spero and the agent, the agent admitted that we were being paid at a lower rate than we should have been—but he didn't care. If we wouldn't accept it, he would employ those that would.

Spero said to us, "He is Mafia. We take him away from people... and we beat him!"

Eventually we settled to be paid at the lower rate—without the use of violence.

Spero had much influence regarding seasonal work in Nafplion. When there wasn't any orange picking available he temporarily found us labouring work at a marble factory.

During mid-February the police started following us to the orchards.

I had known orange pickers who had been jailed. One was a man named Quinn who dressed like a Viking. He received a seven-month sentence for parading a three-foot long sword through town. He only spent a few weeks in prison... A collection was made to enable us to buy Quinn his freedom.

Quinn told me that he spent his time in custody picking oranges in the prison's garden.

Additionally, an English ganger and his girlfriend fought against local men in a cinema... The ganger had his legs broken. Both he and his girlfriend received prison sentences... for fighting!

Towards the end of the season I was unsure of what work to do next. New seasonal workers had arrived from Argos—yet there was little available employment.

While having a drink in a bar known as The Pub, The Top Ganger, aged in his late twenties, and from Liverpool, entered, then asked me if I would be interested in working with him and his girlfriend in Israel. He said that they were going to work on a Moshav. He had met someone who had worked on Moshav Hatzeva—and that the work was well paid. I hardly knew anything of Israel except what I had learned at Sunday School. The Top Ganger continued to persuade me until I agreed to go with them.

CHAPTER FOUR

DURING THE LATTER PART of February, 1982, The Top Ganger, his girlfriend and I waited with others, in anticipation of entering the customs at Ben Gurion Airport. We felt worried due to us having nowhere near the entry requirement of about the equivalent of a few hundred U.S. dollars and a return ticket. Although it would have been cheaper to have arrived in Israel by boat, we were aware that it was a riskier way for those who didn't have enough money. We had met such people in Athens and Nafplion who had gone to Israel by sea, and had been sent back, with a considerable number of passengers, on the same boat.

Although all the monies possessed by the three of us didn't reach two hundred and fifty pounds, I watched people going through the customs who had previously told us that the amount of cash they each had consisted of one pound.

Out of the three of us only The Top Ganger was questioned: he was asked to produce proof of a return air ticket. This he did.

Once in Tel Aviv we joined about thirty others from our flight—and began to look for a cheap place to stay.

Gradually, members of this group went their ways; until only four of us remained.

The three of us and a ginger Manchester man named Mark took a taxi to try and find a hostel we had been given the name of—but ended up getting lost.

Soon after leaving the vehicle. we arrived at a hostel—but it was full. Consequently we were sent to the hostel's annexe where we were allocated a floor to sleep on.

While I slept The Top Ganger returned to the hostel, where he had, by chance, earlier met an old friend from Liverpool.

In the morning I awoke to find a full room. The Top Ganger was angered to find that Mark had gone.

The Top Ganger moaned, "Why didn't he wait? We could have gone together."

The Top Ganger detested being alone… He would sooner be in a triplet than as part of a couple.

As we left the hostel, I was amazed at the number of sleeping people who filled almost every area of space on the floor. Even in the corridor our feet stepped in between necks and arms.

Once outside the hostel we walked to the Moshav office at Leonardo Da Vinci Street.

The Top Ganger told its secretary that we wanted to go to Moshav Hatzeva. His request was granted.

Two women, who were also allocated places there, joined us for refreshments before heading south into The Arava desert, several hours later.

One of the women was from Birmingham and had become short of funds while working on a Kibbutz.

Consequently, she intended to earn enough money to pay her fare home.

The other woman was named Leanne, who was from Australia. She had worked as a waitress in Tolo, a town that was only several miles from Nafplion. She found it to be funny that while it was common for Greek men to have sexual relationships with foreign women, it was extremely rare for non-Greek men to form romantic relationships with Greek women.

Marco had met a young Greek woman who wanted a non-platonic relationship with him; but she feared doing so because she anticipated violence toward her from her father.

Also, while in Nafplion, a Dutchman had been beaten, then chased out of town by the family of a young woman he kissed.

Leanne said that she had a Greek boyfriend—but stressed that all the female tourists who fell for the charm of the Greek men ended up with broken hearts.

After taking a bus journey that took a few hours we arrived on Moshav Hatzeva. Once we had arrived our employers introduced themselves to us.

Uri took me to his home for refreshments.

Subsequently I was taken to a bungalow where I found the living conditions to be good.

I was allocated a room to be shared with my workmate. His name was Wim. He was concerned that the knife-happy drunk who I had replaced would want to reclaim his bed after returning from the bar.

I slept without disturbance. Soon after I had awoken Uri arrived to take me to the office to sort out my paperwork.

The scenery which I hadn't been able to properly observe due to the darkness of the previous night looked so different from anything in real life that I had already seen: the sun blazed at the lifeless looking yellow desert, which was contrasted by the greenness of crops grown in its midst.

After I had been to see the clerk I returned to the bungalow to find that most of its occupants had gone to work; only the person I had replaced remained.

Ian said to me, "I'm going today... you can have my food. The work is just too hard... one day was enough... it was too much for my back."

Ian offered to show me where the supermarket was situated. As we walked, he pointed to the mountains saying, "Jordan... and you'll have to go around the world to get to it."

I felt that he was referring to the fact that it would be permissible to enter Israel via Arab Countries—but not the other way about.

Ian was thirty-four years of age and had previously worked as an industrial diver. After that profession he told me that earnings of seven-hundred pounds a day were made by him selling T-shirts at rock concerts. I even remembered seeing him on television being interviewed... touting tickets at a Rolling Stones concert. Yet he had strained his back on Moshav Hatzeva... working for the equivalent of about three pounds a day.

The realization of how little I would be earning stunned me. While sitting alone I moaned to myself: "What the hell have I done?" I calculated that it would take a couple of months to be able to save the money that it had cost to bring me from Athens—and the additional money to enable me to go to my next place of work outside of Israel.

I returned to my abode—and met the other workers. The person who had been there the longest was a tall Dutchman named Hans. During our conversation, he gave me the impression that not many people remained for long at this Moshav.

Hans also said, "I have a good farmer... your farmer is bad! Uri said to one guy: 'If you stay six months I'll give you an air ticket home.' After six months he asked for his air ticket... and your farmer said, 'I didn't say I would pay for your air ticket!'"

Once the first morning of tomato picking had ended Uri offered me the rest of the day off. This I accepted.

Wim, being, I believe, from London, later arrived back from his day's work, then disgruntingly said, "He didn't give me the afternoon off... on my first day!"

I believe the reason why I had a free afternoon was because Uri didn't want me straining my back—causing him to lose a second worker who only lasted out a day's work.

Hans told me that his farmer had complained that Uri didn't treat his workers well enough, due to him, more often than most employers, having to ask for workers at the Moshav Office. Hans added that a couple of Uri's workers had left without telling him at the optimum picking time of a certain crop. Uri in panic rushed to the farmer of Hans, then pleaded for help. Consequently, Hans and another worker were sent to help him.

During a trip to the Supermarket I met the Birmingham woman whom I had arrived with. She had decided to leave after being there for four days. The work was too hard for her.

Most of the food items were much higher in price than those that I had known in Britain. I realized that I wouldn't be able to save any money unless I ate virtually all my food requirement... having been taken from the fields. My earnings consisted of whatever I had left, if anything, in my supermarket account.

One woman didn't understand this system. On her first trip to the supermarket she filled her trolley with steak, etc. It was later explained to her that she had spent her month's wage during that shopping journey.

I later met Leanne—and she invited me to her abode.

While we took refreshments she told me that her Israeli workmates had admitted to her that all Israeli seasonal workers were paid at twice the rate that non-Israelis were earning.

Since Uri was only growing tomatoes and cucumbers, I realized I'd have to take vegetables from other plots. This was done when we had finished work: I jumped off the tractor—and took egg plants and peppers before jumping back on the mobile vehicle's trailer.

Uri, aged in his early forties, was a mild-mannered man. He was a member of the Israeli Air Force. He sometimes expressed verbal compassion for the Bedouins who had encampments in the nearby desert—whereas Wim, who was also Jewish, hated the Bedouins. He pontificated that the Bedouins shouldn't be in Israel because there was plenty of space for them in Arabic countries.

Wim, being eighteen years old, gave me the impression that he had a good family background in respect of wealth and class. Wim believed that he would become a well-known actor. Wim showed not an element of doubt that he would be famous in the acting business.

Over the past fourteen years I have sometimes watched television and have seen nothing of Wim. Maybe he was, at the time, appearing on another Channel?

Wim decided to finish working on Moshav Hatzeva. Before leaving for Egypt he met his replacement. His name was Steve, who had served as a Sergeant in the British Army.

Steve espoused anti-Semitic comments.

Wim remarked, "I'm Jewish!"

Steve replied, "That's your problem!"

During my time working and sharing a room with Steve, I was told by him that he had come to this Moshav so that he could hide away—due to him having belted a crowbar against the head of a German volunteer at a Kibbutz. He had started strangling Steve, having found him in bed with his girlfriend.

Steve often complained that there weren't enough women on this Moshav. He moaned that it was agony for him to go without having sex for more than a few days.

Later we attended a Moshav party in which Uri was present. Steve attempted to make our boss so drunk—by putting vodka in his orange juice—that Uri wouldn't be able to take us to work so early in the morning.

Steve was approached by a young woman in a way which I feel could have eventuated in romance as we walked from the party; but he wasn't interested in such a relationship.

I asked him, "Why didn't you go off with her?"

He retorted, "I'm a married man"—even though he had previously said that he was single.

Just before five the next morning, we realized that Steve's party trick hadn't worked—on seeing Uri driving his tractor over the sands.

Hans shouted at him through a window, "Go away!"

Steve, like the rest of us, found the work to be very hard; but he tried to get out of doing it through hiding and pretending to be ill.

He also discovered that food had to be hidden. He had found that someone had taken the cheese that he stored in the fridge. He said to a German volunteer, "I'll break your fingers if you take my cheese again!"

I once arrived at my abode to find foreign teeth marks on my bread!

Hans commented to a Scotsman, whose original profession was as his own—a teacher—on seeing him breakfast on sugared bread and water, "Ian... you are not a prisoner... you know!"

But we *were* prisoners... of poverty!

There was a sense of forced solitude on Moshav Hatzeva... It was so difficult to know workers in other bungalows. I had hardly seen anything of The Top Ganger and his girlfriend. I sometimes saw them working in a distant field.

On a chance meeting, the three of us decided to meet on Wednesdays at the bar.

Over the weeks we spoke of many things. The Top Ganger had previously done seasonal work in France and Belgium—but the place that he was most fond of was Friday Bridge Camp.

On one of the few times that I visited my friends they surprised me by presenting me with a tea, to celebrate my birthday. Consequently I promised to sing on the Top Ganger's girlfriend's birthday at Friday Bridge Camp.

My friends said that their employer was fairly good to work for; but on the whole there seemed to be more bad employers than good ones!

A Scotsman named Gordon arrived on Moshav Hatzeva—to enable him to save enough money for himself and a friend to be able to go to Portugal. He and his friend had tossed a coin to decide which of them was to work on a Moshav.

Gordon toiled for more hours in a day than anyone else that I knew of on Moshav Hatzeva. During one morning Gordon started to work in the fields at 5.30 a.m.—and finished his day doing factory work until midnight. He was rewarded with a lie in bed until 7.00 a.m. on the following morning.

Gordon lived predominantly on a diet of rice, yet he often worked between twelve and fourteen hours a day. He had actually worked in Jordan with some other volunteers. This land had been taken by this Moshav as its own.

Some volunteers had blown a wheel off their jeep… after drunkenly driving over one of the landmines that protected this settlement from Arab attack.

After a month's work, Gordon was given a present by his employer, being the equivalent of thirty pounds.

Ian and Hans worked together for between six and nine hours a day. Ian was given the equivalent of one hundred U.S. dollars—as a present from his farmer for a month's work. Hans had arrived in Israel without any money after travelling through Turkey, Syria, and Jordan. He was given a bonus of the equivalent of three hundred U.S. dollars and presents from his farmer.

Some workers had such good employers that they returned to work for them each year.

One of the best paid workers I was aware of worked five hours a day.

Certain volunteers earned comparatively good money in the irrigation gang, but there weren't many positions available.

Uri had given the same leaving gift to both Wim and Steve: two packets of cigarettes.

Steve finished working on Moshav Hatzeva after being there for three weeks—and had worked considerably more hours in each week than Hans and Ian had!

Steve's replacement was most different from him. His name was Jeremy—a garrulous former public schoolboy who I believe originated from Surrey. I found him to be a genuine, cultured man—whom I would have been prepared to trust to a larger extent than I would most other people.

Jeremy began working with me during the back end of the tomato season. On travelling across the desert to work, Jeremy commented, "Isn't that a dramatic sunrise!"—as the orange sunrays flushed the sky from behind the Jordan mountains; but having seen the same sight for so many dawns, my aesthetic appreciation of natural beauty had been nullified—through tiredness.

The melon crop was the last one that I harvested—which was so much easier to do than working on the tomatoes and cucumbers. One morning we arrived for work to find that some watermelons had been clawed apart. On a shell there were two teeth marks... There were also fist-sized sand prints, indicative of a big cat.

Uri informed the Moshav hunter, who drove in a jeep with a rifle into the desert—but the animal in question wasn't found.

After two months since arriving on Hatzeva, for the first time, The Top Ganger and his girlfriend arrived at my abode. They asked me what my plans were. I said I was going to stay for a couple more weeks before going to work on a kibbutz.

The two of them were returning to Friday Bridge Camp in anticipation of planting work. His parting words to me were, "Don't be surprised if you're asked to be a ganger when you go back to the camp."

The three of us had over the past two months met other people whom we had recognized in Nafplion.

I had heard many complaints about life on Moshav Hatzeva—but the most unusual one I was made aware of was by a young northern Englishman who said he didn't like it because it wasn't the same as Manchester.

Before I left Moshav Hatzeva, I met, for the third time since I arrived, Leanne. Leanne was so proud that she had lasted for ten weeks… after so many workers had finished prematurely… and had saved enough money to go to her next destination. Leanne went to collect her savings at the safe in the Secretary's office she kept with her workmates. To her horror, Leanne discovered that her British workmate whom she regarded a friend had visited the office earlier and had taken her money as well as his own. Leanne was devastated.

CHAPTER FIVE

I ARRIVED at the Kibbutz office at Sutine Street—to see a woman and a big bearded man.

Whilst starting a conversation regarding Kibbutzim, the woman interrupted my speech by saying, "Why don't you go to kibbutz Hukuk?"

The man said, "I'll take you. There are fourteen Scandinavian girls and you can drink beer every night!"

I responded, "I'll go!"

While the Secretary did my paperwork, the man whose name was pronounced as Shooki asked me to accompany him for a drive about Tel Aviv.

We visited factories where he ordered supplies for his kibbutz.

After he bought me refreshments, I was taken back to Sutine Street. The office was locked; but on a seat outside its door I found my passport—which could have been picked up by anyone walking past it.

Soon after arriving at Kibbutz Hukuk, ending a picturesque drive through some green mountains of Northern Israel, I realized I had been conned: there weren't fourteen

Scandinavian females present—it was like a home for retired bachelors!

My accommodation was in an old shack-like building which I shared with a big New Yorker named Geoff.

Geoff told me that he had been ill—and hadn't worked for a fortnight—but was presently pretending to be sick to avoid doing any work.

During my first sleep I heard Geoff and a Frenchwoman speak about me.

I found the cordial singing of birds during the arrival of the next light to have awoken me in a different way that I had known on Hatzeva. There, the hints of the approaching soundless sun awoke me.

I was allocated work in the dining room, banana plantation and cotton fields... But, on average, I spent half the time at work as I did on Hatzeva.

I didn't really know what to do with so much spare time.

Some volunteers spent their time at tea parties, whilst others could be found at the bar and swimming pool—or partaking in sports—and visiting nearby Tiberias.

Also, I didn't have to prepare my own meals: all meals were prepared for us.

While eating in the dining room someone kissed the right side of my face. I turned to see a Downs syndrome child. It was a touching encounter... It was one of the few times in my life that I had been voluntarily kissed.

There was a much more friendly and relaxed atmosphere on Hukuk than on Hatzeva—where the theft of food and tension caused through tiredness and impoverishment tended to exhibit some of the negative aspects in people.

During the five weeks I was on Hukuk new people arrived and long-term volunteers left—plus, some didn't stay for a day because they didn't like the accommodation that was usually allocated to new arrivals.

The volunteers were French, Irish, British, Australasians, North and South Americans and a Russian.

I replaced a long staying volunteer at an area of Hukuk known as the fortress. My room there was a lot better than my initial abode. I liked the old character of the fortress. We also had a pet snake that lived in the garden.

Some French volunteers were told to leave Hukuk by Dina the volunteer leader—for taking advantage of the Kibbutz system without wanting to support it through doing work.

One of them was a former heroin addict named Herve— who gave me the impression that he considered most things to be a joke.

Hukuk was like Hatzeva in the respect that I found no evidence of religion.

The kindly middle-aged volunteer leader said to me, "I'm an atheist." Her anguished face indicated to me the suffering she had known due to her son having been killed at war.

On working by Capernum, near the Sea of Galilee, doing irrigation work on the cotton plant, I did think of Jesus Christ. The Israelis I spoke to about Jesus hardly knew anything of this famous historical figure.

Geoff had told me about rats in the banana plantation... I thought he was joking. He tickled, from behind, my shoulder while I carried a bunch.

On placing a very heavy bunch on my shoulder a large Israeli man screamed. About an inch away from my hand jumped a massive grey rat.

The leader of the banana gang was known as Cheeky. Cheeky said to me, "What are you worried about? A rat isn't a tiger!"

The volunteers didn't have a lot of contact with the Israelis… apart from work. The Israelis seemed to live quiet lives on the kibbutz—which was such a contrast from their military experiences. One of the banana gang had been a member of the squad that had stormed the hijacked plane in Entebbe, while another member of Kibbutz Hukuk was a commander of an elite force.

A young Russian volunteer told me that he had escaped from Russia with his parents. His name was Gadi.

I asked him what life in Russia had been like.

He replied, "It was terrible!"

I then asked, "Would you ever return?"

Gadi returned after a pause, "Yes… as a spy!"

I also met on Kibbutz Hukuk a woman named Isobel who was from Norfolk. We became friends… and still are.

CHAPTER SIX

I RETURNED to Friday Bridge Camp during early July 1982. I had returned because I wanted to be a ganger.

I was put in a hut that was occupied by Andy. While he lay on a bed I gave a packet of Greek cigarettes—then partially filled his tin mug with whisky—as we conversed.

I liked Andy because he didn't pretend to be anything that he wasn't. Since knowing him previously at Friday Bridge Camp and in Nafplion I was aware that little restraint was needed to stop him from playing a dirty trick on someone that had done him a favour. The dirty deeds that he had done to people, including his friends, were well recited by those who knew him.

In the evening I went with Andy to the club.

While there I put a packet of cigarettes into Ken's hand before shaking it. While we talked, I watched the Top Ganger converse with the courgette boss as they looked in my direction.

I saw the heavy personality of the courgette boss walking towards me. He proffered a hand for me to shake. With a smile, and a voice that was persuasive, he said, "Will you take a gang out in the morning? I'd be very grateful."

"All right," I returned.

Initially I only ganged on a temporary basis, in which I picked strawberries on some alternative days; and, on one day my name wasn't on the list. I complained to Ken that I wasn't happy about this.

He retorted, "Look at your face... you've worked four days in a week... and you're complaining that you're not working tomorrow... and there's campers who don't work at all!"

Later, the courgette boss said to me, "If ever your name isn't on the worklist... make your own way to the fields."

This I did; but I knew I had to keep away from the roads—because I was aware that two of the van drivers were informers. The information that they had previously relayed to the labour officer had caused work-seeking campers to have been ordered off the camp. So I went to Laddus through the fields behind the camp to work in Marco's gang.

After several days on the camp I was made a full-time ganger. The Top Ganger made a place for me. I replaced a former soldier known as Wigan Willie on the basis that The Top Ganger had a grudge against him.

Joe the foreman, whom I had known last year, had committed suicide. A local told me that Joe's father and brothers had also killed themselves.

Joe was replaced by the German tractor driver named Gus.

I had worked with him a year earlier—collecting full crates—and delivering empty ones.

I much preferred being a ganger than a cutter, not just because I was to be paid more, but because the time seemed to go faster, due to an increase in concentration that was necessary to work efficiently. Also, I got to know more and more campers due to my gang's workers changing from day to day.

One worker was a young man from Liverpool who anticipated doing a degree in science at Cambridge University. He had achieved five grade A A-levels.

Another cutter in my gang was a retired journalist who had once worked on *The Daily Mail* newspaper.

Also, some staff members on their day off would spend that time cutting in my gang. I found the breakfast cook, who was aged sixty, to be more suited to land work than catering. I found him to have been a good agricultural worker—but not so good at hygienically preparing food.

Sometimes a few of the gangers were sent with their gangs to work at the headquarters of the courgette boss—where we were employed doing indoor work topping and tailing corn—and transporting young pheasants from pen to pen.

While topping and tailing corn, Bald Alan worked for a day in my gang. He said to me regarding my position, "While you are of use you will be treated well... when you are of no more use you will be brushed aside like a piece of shit!"

Also, John the Cowboy cut in my gang. He joked, "When I'm paid I feel like giving the money back... for the amount of work I've done!"

But, having worked with him two years earlier at Shippey's on the Windfallen apples, I knew him to have been an outstanding worker; yet, I couldn't give the same compliment to him regarding the courgettes. Having watched him crush vegetables and plants as his powerful trunk rushed through the rows I feel that it would have been justifiable for him to have paid the courgette boss!

The courgette boss had become the Chairman of Friday Bridge Camp... and the food had become worse. Yet the courgette boss during this season frequented the dining hall more often than last season, giving the impression: we cannot complain, he's eating this junk himself!

The courgette boss joined the gangers at their breakfast table and told the most humourless and childish jokes that I had heard recited by an adult. He then watched those who laughed. At a table away from us sat a woman who looked to be twenty years older than me and seventy pounds heavier.

The courgette boss said to me, "She'd be all right for you."

I also found him awkward to work for: even though I was a ganger, he continued to pay me a cutter's wage.

Each Friday, at pay time, I addressed him and said, "I want my money."

His reply was similar for each of the times I asked him. He insincerely responded, "I'll look after you."

The last time I requested the money I was owed, he offhandedly retorted, "You can always go plumbing."

But, I realized from his answer that he had the same knowledge as me, in the respect that the plum crop was very bad. After three weeks he paid me all that he owed me.

During my birthday on Moshav Hatzeva I had promised to sing on the stage at the camp for The Top Ganger's girlfriend on her birthday.

The entertainment officer visited different people in the audience of about four hundred.

I said to him as he compiled the list of acts, "Mike, don't put me on first... put me in the middle."

As I watched in between rows of excited locals and campers to the stage, Mike announced, "And, for the first act of the night, Mr John Mallon... guitarist extraordinaire!"

I cannot play a guitar. I trembled as I walked through the cheers and went onto the stage. I then whispered to Daisy, the seventy-year-old pianist, the song I was to sing.

I began to use the microphone... listening to my horrible voice being fed back through this instrument.

My performance was so bad that the audience demanded an encore!

I spontaneously attacked a number that I hadn't rehearsed before leaving the stage.

Subsequently a young English Physics undergraduate named Graham who shared a hut with myself, Andy and others, approached me, then said, "I will support you... and our hut."

He magnificently sang a Romeo and Juliet piece—and was booed off the stage.

One night in the disco... being adjacent to the clubhouse... some local skinheads entered... then, one of them made an advance to Scottish Norma while another did the same to The Top Ganger's girlfriend. Consequently, fighting took place between the skinheads, gangers and some staff members.

Soon after the skinheads had left the camp Bald Alan said, "They'll be back."

Scottish Norma had been taking a shower—and saw a pair of eyes looking at her. Those eyes she recognized. She subsequently made a complaint to the labour officer—being supported by the evidence of some other staff members.

They were told to go away. The man under determination was a senior staff member.

Consequently, vile graffiti was written about this senior staff member on the gangers' toilet walls.

Later the labour officer warned that if the gangers continued using such graffiti they would be in trouble!

Scottish Norma and South African Selina had fallen out with The Top Ganger. Both of them being blonde and physically attractive, they were paid at a ganger's rate, to travel with the courgette boss in his Mercedes to the fields each morning—where they then put out knives and buckets.

The Top Ganger stormed, "It's not fair! they should have the same pay as gangers." He demanded that all the gangers stopped talking to them.

Selina's boyfriend, Mick, was particularly upset— because he had been a member of The Top Gangers' clique since 1980 and had given him extra food from the cookhouse.

Selina had been the best strawberry picker on the camp during this season—so grudges would have been levelled at

her for earning too much money—especially since 1982 was
the first time she had been on Friday Bridge Camp.

Mick had been fortunate to have been able to work in the
cookhouse during the 1982 season.

A place was made for him by a friend of his who put up a
sign in the area where staff members dined, stating that 'The
Head Barman and The Head Woman are like pigs—Signed
Scouse Dave.' Even though Dave didn't compose this sign,
he was sacked—and threatened with violence.

Mick used to bath in the dish sink before starting the
afternoon shift. Bodna, being in charge of the cooking,
didn't mind this. Bodna and his second in command, Steve,
had been Prisoners of War in East Anglia. They didn't return
to Eastern Europe but arrived at Friday Bridge Camp soon
after the Second World War and had remained there.

One morning some campers arrived at the cookhouse in a
worried state. They said that a camper in their hut had been
ill throughout the night.

Joe went to their hut and arrived just before the twenty-
four year old Englishman died.

A member of his hut later told me that the sick man had
cried in anguish through the early hours. They had tried
unsuccessfully to get help on the camp... and being
foreigners, they didn't know how to telephone local medical
centres. They had to wait until 4.30 a.m. until catering staff
members had arrived for work.

I found that work on the courgette beds throughout most
of the season to have been disharmonious.

Gus had rankled most of the gangers more than once. He differed from the courgette boss in the respect that he believed gangers should cut as well. I agreed with the boss... A dyke consisted of thousands of dumped courgettes that had lost their worth because they had grown too big due to the rows not being checked by the gangers.

Courgette cutters at Friday Bridge

Marco got sacked for neglecting his beds. He had said that they didn't need cutting.

Mac the lorry driver suspiciously cut through a small part of a row—and got a few buckets of vegetables that should have been taken a week sooner.

The Burmese man maintained that his beds belonged to some other gangers; but this explanation did him no good.

During that week the camp lost two gangers; Marco's girlfriend who was also a ganger left as well.

During a morning's work I told my workers they would have to work faster. They ignored me as they slowly cut through the bed.

At 10.00 a.m. one of them said, "It's break time."

I retorted, "You're going back to the camp."

They complained, "You didn't give us a chance!"

I returned, "I told you once... and, you refused to work sufficiently."

At break time I felt so important while gangers and cutters talked about what I did!

The Top Ganger grinned as he walked to where I sat, then said, "You sacked your whole gang?"

"Yes," I returned.

Once The Top Ganger departed from me an Italian camper arrived, then pleaded with me, "Please give me a chance."

"No... I told you, once!"

Once the Italian had gone, another ganger named Brian came, then said, "You shouldn't have sacked them! You couldn't even look him in the eye as he asked you for a chance! You might have fooled everyone else but I can see through you!"

Maybe Brian could see that I also sacked them because I wanted to make a name for myself?

I was like a socialist in the waiting... yearning to learn Thatcherism at its most unfair advantage.

Brian was the ganger that I got on with the least; our divergent perceptions of reality allowed our personalities to have the miscibility of ionic and covalent liquids.

We shared the same hut and disagreed on virtually everything that we conversed on.

I didn't dislike him... and Brian said he liked me because he liked bores.

I later philosophised: Even though I am a bore, surely everyone else must be a bore to someone.

Incidentally, that sacked Italian, on another day, returned to work for me. I found it difficult to stop him for a break. He went through the rows like a rabbit.

Andy had also become a ganger and, I feel he was like me... in the respect that this position had gone to his head.

Unbeknown to Andy he could have been a ganger in 1981. The courgette boss had asked The Top Ganger whether he thought it was a good idea to make Andy a ganger. The Top Ganger said no. He justified his answer by saying that Andy would desert the courgettes once the apples had started.

The Top Ganger privately said to me the reason why he had said no was because he couldn't bear seeing campers grovelling to Andy for work.

The Top Ganger, though, did do Andy a favour, in 1981. The courgette boss wanted to throw Andy off the camp, for desertion. He justified his motive, saying that Andy was one of several campers that had regular work on the courgettes— then, once the apples had started, he would deserted him for a better paid job. The Top Ganger used his diplomatic influence to stop having his friend made to leave the camp.

Another member of my hut was also a ganger. His name was Beverley, who I had known on Moshav Hatzeva. He was nicknamed Mr British, due to him having the characteristics of an officer who upheld the will of the British Empire during the nineteenth century in some colony.

Beverley differed from the other gangers in the respect that he was pedantically culture-conscious. He had done so much in terms of travelling—and felt disappointed because people on the camp considered him to be a bore. His know-all attitude gave him the air of a youth hostel sage.

Beverley's conversation suggested to me that he regarded himself to be both a Socialist and a monarchist. I felt that he did seasonal work so as to finance travel in foreign countries; whereas we did seasonal work in one place... and, then, subsequently did seasonal work somewhere else. We were not concerned about social and cultural systems of foreign countries, being interested in things like how much alcohol our wages would buy.

Whilst at work, Beverley cut through his row before the rest of his gang had done theirs, so he practised on his cricket... bowling a worthless round courgette while waiting for the rest of his gang to reach him.

After spectating his bowling Gus sacked him.

Beverley bitterly responded, "The trouble with Germans is they're okay until they put on uniforms... then they just have to be the boss!"

The only thing that I was aware of in which the gangers liked Gus for was that he unintentionally gave them more wage tickets; these were cashed in on Fridays.

The workers in one gang had to chase after their ganger to get their tickets.

This ganger had told me that he was interested in doing an armed robbery on the courgette boss as he drove the weekly wages to the office at the camp.

Another ganger spent some of his Saturdays shoplifting in Peterborough. He later left agriculture work to start a career in the Police Force.

The Top Ganger had the reputation of being the fastest courgette cutter... He did, when I worked in his gang, usually finish his row before the next quickest worker reached the halfway mark.

During a day's work, The Top Ganger and I worked our gangs on the same bed. We worked from opposite ends until we met in the middle. The last section to be harvested was a row which I shared with The Top Ganger. We worked at opposite sides of this row. Instead of stopping once we met I continued cutting and harvested seventeen courgettes that should have been cut!

Shock was on The Top Gangers face, on seeing that I had rumbled his deliberate neglect—which I believe he did so he would be able to say 'Look at me—I'm the first out of the row!' I found it comical that the most trusted ganger—who acted as a medium between us and the courgette boss—had caused more damage than any other worker on the courgette beds. Gangers like Marco had been caught doing the same thing, and accordingly dealt with—but Gus never checked The Top Ganger's beds.

Soon after discovering The Top Ganger's negligence a new ganger's rule was announced: Gangers shouldn't check other gangers' beds!

Occasionally I met Tom at The Sportsman. He had continued to work for the same farmer since 1980 doing apple picking. Tom had a free place to live; and every other week he earned fourteen pounds a day and picked for seven days. But, for a few days every alternative week, he visited Barnsley to sign for unemployment and housing benefits. Tom justified this, saying that he had attempted being honest in 1980 but was refused unemployment benefit with myself... for being gypsies and had decided that when dealing with the social security honesty didn't pay!

During the season The Labour Officer asked me if I wanted to work on a Saturday.

I asked, "What is it?"

He stormed, "See the worklist." He then abruptly walked away from me.

I looked at the worklist to see that my name wasn't on it. The work was apple picking at Rockcliffe's. Mostly courgette gangers' names were listed.

The Labour Officer was considerably quieter this season. During last winter he had been rushed to hospital suffering from cirrhosis of the liver.

He did however shout at a Nafplion ganger who had arrived at the camp: "Piss off!"—even though it was the first time he had ever seen him!

During the season Shaun and Mervin came to work on the camp. We agreed to return to Nafplion together. Andy behaved like he had done a year earlier, promising people jobs and threatening another that he would make sure he wouldn't receive any work in Nafplion.

Ken said to me, "He's at it again promising people jobs... and you saw what he was like in Greece."

Andy was obsessed with Greece... No matter what subject we conversed on, he always changed it to Greece.

One wet Sunday afternoon I entered our hut, to find Andy wearing a red bobble hat and sunglasses, dancing on his bed, and drinking Greek wine to the accompaniment of Greek music.

I had known Andy to have chelated at least one rough, drunken woman to our hut. He didn't care who heard their loud rude noises whereas other members of our hut were more discreet.

Brian said regarding our privileged positions, "The working class can kiss my arse... I've got the ganger's job at last!"

During this season I met a Coventry woman named Claire whom I had made friends with at the camp in 1981... and we are still friends.

CHAPTER SEVEN

SHAUN, MERVIN, MY BROTHER DAVID and I entered an Athens-bound coach at Victoria Station, London. On the bus we journeyed with others from Friday Bridge Camp that I hadn't anticipated meeting: The Top Ganger, Little Al and Humberside Pete.

There was a mild tenseness between Mervin and The Top Ganger due to them being rival gangers in 1980 on the courgettes, I believe. Yet both of them exhibited a light cordiality to one another as the vehicle moved through a November evening of 1982.

The Top Ganger reached down a couple of rows and squeezed the bottom of a woman who searched the luggage rack, making the impression that Pete, who sat opposite her, had done it! Pete squirmed in embarrassment as if believing that his face was about to be slapped.

The woman under determination sat down as if the incident hadn't arisen.

In Yugoslavia the Greek driver got into a fight with a bar owner. The lights of the bar went out. Its staff tried to stop people from leaving without paying their bills. The Top Ganger pushed his way out.

**A drink in the Travellers Rest, Victoria before the 3 day
bus trip to Athens**

A couple of days after arriving in Nafplion, Mervin
complained that it was not the same as last year—so he was
going home.

Shaun decided to go with him. I liked Shaun: he was an
easy-going popular man, who had been doing seasonal work
for a few years—after being made redundant at Ebbw Vale
Steel Works aged in his mid-forties.

The Top Ganger responded, regarding their departure,
"When things go wrong for Mervin—everyone has to
suffer!"

I met with some other people whom I had previously
known, but not in Nafplion. These were Joe and Mick who

had worked on the staff at Friday Bridge Camp; and Scouse Stevie and Toti who had been campers in 1980.

They had arrived in Nafplion before us and, due to there being a lack of work, the four of them spent their days fishing in the Mediterranean.

Joe said, "There was no work for illegal people because there were too many unemployed Greeks."

I responded, "I might as well go to Israel."

Joe retorted, "Don't say that. I don't want you to go."

"What are we going to do?" added Stevie in a panicky voice.

I later spoke with Ken about the work situation. He said, "It will be all right, you'll see."

Within a few days Spero returned and seemed glad to see some of last season's seasonal workers in town.

My employment in Spero's gang was brief. The Lebanese ganger was deported.

As the days went by more people who had worked at Friday Bridge Camp arrived in town—such as Andy, Big Al, Big Jim, Norma, Selina, Bald Alan and his girlfriend. They blended into various gangs with others from the camp.

Andy managed to become a ganger.

He got into a fight with the boyfriend of a woman he sacked so as to make room for his friends.

Andy didn't remain a ganger: his gang members became so fed up with him that they sacked him.

I managed to find work in a gang run by a tall Greek named Barri. His gang was well organised—and the pay was better than in other gangs I had worked in overall.

Dutch Mike also joined this gang, being big, blond and arrogant. He was dismissive of most of the workers in town and often criticised pickers who weren't able to harvest anywhere near as many oranges as he could. He publicly humiliated one worker, accusing him of pretending to be an orange... instead of working.

During a December evening three gangs of orange pickers travelled in the back of a lorry along the Argos road to Nafplion. These gangs were headed by Barri and French Patrick.

The truck suddenly halted. A torch was then shone in on us. A middle-aged policeman asked, "Who are you?"

"We're hitchhikers," answered one of twenty-seven people—who wore working clothes and muddy footwear, while some of us ate oranges.

He responded, "I'm taking you to the station."

As the vehicle accelerated we decided to vacate it. French Patrick descended first—just as the velocity of the truck sharply increased, causing him to land painfully on his posterior.

The remainder cautiously left the vehicle—then split up into groups.

I returned to Nafplion along the coast with Mick who had worked as a staff member at Friday Bridge Camp.

On the following day Barri explained the motive regarding the police: "All they wanted was money for Christmas... it was then okay."

Another gang I heard about was also stopped by police. Once they had been taken to the Police Station they were warned that if caught working again they would be deported. An hour after leaving the station they returned to work.

James' gang

I decided to change gangs... Dutch Mike joined me in Spanish Jiame's gang.

During the morning break Mike challenged Jiame's leadership—and gave him orders.

Jiame returned, "I am the ganger."

Mike retorted: "When you can pick as much as me, then you are the ganger."

At the end of the first day I was asked if I would stay in this gang. I accepted, while Mike was told by the ganger that there was no place in it for him.

I enjoyed working in Jiame's gang—not just because the people in it were the best gang of pickers that I had worked with, and because Jiame was such a good ganger—but because there was such a fun-loving atmosphere in it, and we socialized together in the evenings. It was also pleasant to be away from Friday Bridge people. On the courgette fields gangers had spoken much about Greece; and in Nafplion the same people talked a lot about Friday Bridge Camp.

The most impressive picker that I saw in Jiame's gang was a man from Central Africa named Phillipe.

Also, what I liked about Jiame's gang was that we worked regularly. Its agent Costa made sure that we always had good food.

One morning at a new farm the farmer said that since his wife was ill we wouldn't be having a meal.

Jiame said to him that we wouldn't pick his oranges unless we had a cooked dinner and wine.

The farmer left us. He later returned to say that his wife had recovered, and Jiame's request was granted.

A farmer's role was different in Greece than it was in East Anglia. We hardly had any contact with Greek farmers. They just provided food, wine and places to work. We were paid through an agent who was employed by a factory. Costa earned enough money during the two to three months he worked as an agent that he was able to take the remainder of the year off.

While at Friday Bridge Camp I had worked for several farmers, but I have no idea of the number of Greek farms I worked on. I worked on so many. Sometimes we worked for just a day at an orchard—and a few days on another—but rarely more than several days were spent picking oranges at the same place.

We had no trouble being paid by Costa, but one other gang wasn't as fortunate as us.

A gang member told me that at the end of a day's work on a farm its owner refused to pay them. He said that another gang member threatened to set his car on fire.

The owner threatened to shoot gang members with a hand gun that he aimed at them.

Consequently they reported this incident to the police.

The police responded, "Don't bother with him... He shot someone last year!"

A Yugoslavian woman named Nana, who was a former girlfriend of Dutch Mike's, visited the Captain of Police and asked him for a work permit. He refused, but offered her a job picking oranges for his uncle.

Dutch Mike's new girlfriend was Greek, and her friend, who was of the same nationality, went out with Burnley Mick. These women originated from one of the islands.

Dutch Mike and other members of the gang they were in became the highest paid orange pickers in Nafplion. They were paid at a very high rate to collect frost-damaged oranges. This employment was paid through subsidies from the Greek Government to farmers.

Dutch Mike, my brother David, Nobber and others entered a bar I was in, then said that they had earned 4,300 drachmas for a day's work. This was an incredibly high wage... Most of the gangs I was aware of made less than 2,000 drachmas a day.

Dutch Mike and other gang members were employed by a gypsy. They went to his encampment for payment—and were told he was away. They later returned to find that the whole encampment had moved to an unknown region.

I hadn't met a gypsy before working in Greece. In Greece these nomadic people were gypsies by race: Romany. In Wisbech gypsies were defined as any scruffy people living in caravans.

I was surprised by the sudden way in which severe frosts had prematurely ended the orange season. During this time Dutch Mike was arrested for robbing a cafe.

On the morning that I became convinced the oranges had ended my brother and I went back to Athens.

While staying at Festos, someone repeatedly whispered my name—outside my room. I opened the door to see The Top Ganger. He asked me if I would accompany him and some other Friday Bridge people on a boat they would be taking to Israel. I refused. I had reached the stage where I wanted to do new things with different people.

CHAPTER EIGHT

I **ARRIVED IN BEN GURION** airport on a weekend during the latter part of January 1983. I found sleeping at this airport to be comfortless.

Once I had returned from a bathroom visit I found that one of my plastic bags holding some of my belongings was missing.

Once I had returned from a second bathroom visit I saw that my bag had returned...without anything being taken from it.

On the Monday morning after the weekend of my arrival I went to the Kibbutz Office at Leonardo Da Vinci Street.

A young woman allocated me a place at Kibbutz Haogen.

Since this settlement was only situated 29 kms north of Tel Aviv, I was able to arrive there during the same morning.

Once I had done my paperwork the volunteer leader introduced me to my sleeping area. She subsequently took me to the dining hall where I ate with other volunteers. While eating I recognized a woman I had known on Kibbutz Hukuk—and a man who had worked on the oranges in Greece.

I subsequently met my roommates: Maurice and Greg.

As the days went by I found Maurice to be a modest, easy to get on with person. In some of his spare time Maurice wrote his Ph.D. thesis, which, I believe, was on a branch of mechanical engineering. Kibbutz Haogen held an attraction for him because it was known as the Runners' Kibbutz... Maurice participated in running. He trained with the Israeli running champion, who lived on Haogen. Maurice originated from Pudsey and was patriotic to various aspects of Yorkshire life. Maurice said that Yorkshire was the only place where he was willing to settle.

Greg was very different from Maurice. Maurice rationalized with the logic of a scientist, whereas Greg, who originated from Birmingham, Alabama, used metaphysical concepts in his reasoning. He had been on another kibbutz and intended going to India in search of his guru.

I had told Greg during work in an orange orchard that I was considering training to be a boxing referee.

Greg volunteered to give me some practice—by randomly challenging a man to a boxing contest.

I got on well with my roommates—but Maurice didn't get along with Greg as well as he did with me. Maurice, being a non-smoker, had requested for volunteers who didn't smoke to be placed in his room. Although Greg had informed the volunteer leader that he didn't smoke, cigarettes were puffed by him in our room.

Greg often awoke the first—and Maurice being down to earth found on awakening it odd to see Greg meditating on his bed with a white sheet covering him.

Before leaving Kibbutz Haogen Maurice had become a hero: he defeated the Israeli champion in a televised race.

When the two of them trained together it was the champion who usually won but during the event that mattered most, Maurice prevailed.

Maurice returned to Yorkshire in anticipation of doing seasonal work in Norway.

Although Greg was Jewish, some kibbutz officials wanted him to leave Haogen—especially the volunteer leader who seemed to be confounded by his behaviour.

Whilst working at the plastics factory he practised martial arts—as he waited for rolls to be produced. Greg justified his actions by saying that he didn't waste time.

I had heard the volunteer leader say that she couldn't stand Americans. This surprised me since America was supportive of the Israeli economy. I later concluded that her attitude was formed by the drug-damaged American volunteers and ulpanists—who weren't able to make a positive contribution to the kibbutz system. But her way of thinking didn't appear to take into account the good American workers who did not have drug problems.

Soon after I had arrived on this settlement I was requested by the volunteer leader to attend a meeting. It was about a person I hadn't met. He was a New Yorker who had been ordered to leave the kibbutz for possessing drugs.

A New York Jew named Howard was also ordered to leave.

I had watched him during one evening grinning—as he stared at the cows in the paddock opposite the volunteers' quarters. On entering and leaving my room a couple of times during that night, spanning a few hours, I was aware of

Howard standing at the same spot using the same facial expression.

While working with him in an orchard he whispered in a secretive way to me, even though no-one was near enough to have heard our conversation irrespective of how loudly we spoke.

The volunteer leader checked up on Howard. She discovered that he had been made to leave his last kibbutz due to him peddling drugs.

After leaving Kibbutz Haogen, Howard went to Tel Aviv. There, he emptied his luggage at a roadside, then stripped himself naked before lying down.

He was committed to an institution for the mentally ill.

Eventually Greg left Haogen voluntarily. He returned to his old kibbutz.

My new roommates were a Swede named Connie and a Lancashire man named Steve.

Connie had travelled through Asia, Europe and North America. While in India he worked with Mother Teresa. Some of his friends were people I had known at Friday Bridge Camp. He had come to this kibbutz for the same reason as I had done—to relax in an easy-going environment for a while.

Steve had arrived on this kibbutz before me, but had decided to change rooms. He had no interest in Israeli culture and didn't care who owned the Holy Land. The prospect of romance and parties were the aspects that attracted him mostly to work on a kibbutz. Steve abhorred sunshine and went to bed while other volunteers relished the prospect of swimming in the nearby sea and swimming pool—and after eight months in Israel this frail ginger volunteer's skin was as pale as lime water. Steve rarely went from this settlement; one of the few times that he left Kibbutz Haogen was to sell a watch at the Arab market in Jerusalem.

Steve refused to speak with me for five days—due to an Israeli woman he'd been unsuccessfully trying to romance had decided to speak to Connie.

Steve worked in the kitchen and plastics factory and refused to work outdoors because of his bad leg, yet, dressed as Superman, he danced for most of the night at parties.

His occasional dancing partner, being ten inches taller than him at six foot four, was a New Yorker named Mary. Mary told me that she worked for two months a year in Alaska in a fish processing factory. The four thousand dollars that she saved enabled her to travel for the rest of each year.

Steve's vulnerable personality attracted the sympathies of two American born-again Christians named Charlie and James. They secretly held bible classes because the teaching of religion was banned on Kibbutz Haogen. They persuaded Steve to be baptized—at an arranged ceremony in Tiberius, but he changed his mind because it coincided with my birthday party.

They asked him, "What is the most important, God... or John's party?" He replied, "John's party." Consequently they called him Judas.

Eventually Steve was forcibly removed from Haogen for the same reason he had been ordered to leave his previous settlement—this volunteer was too dependent on kibbutz life.

Charlie and James openly confessed to us their bad pasts. Charlie had been a drug pusher, while James belonged to a Hell's Angel chapter,

A thirty-five year old man named Doug responded, "You notice one thing about born-again Christians... they all claim to have previously been bad people."

What Doug and I had in common was that we had a practical knowledge of East Anglia: whilst I had been on Friday Bridge Camp, he was a native of East Anglia.

Doug said of his own people, "They are an inward looking people who dislike outsiders." Hostility was shown to him when returning home, because he had travelled so much. Doug had worked about the world for much of his adult life—and held a wide knowledge of inhabitants in different cultures—but he wasn't culturally condescending. His bespectacled academic appearance gave him the air of an early twentieth-century British archaeologist. Doug used the largest vocabulary of anyone I had known. We become friends... and our friendship has continued.

Doug, who isn't Jewish, initially worked as a volunteer before becoming an ulpanist—so as to learn Hebrew. I was surprised that Doug, being older than thirty, was able to work as a volunteer.

A Californian ulpanist named Rena said that her father, at the age of fifty-seven, worked as a volunteer on another kibbutz.

The ulpanists were generally regarded to be troublesome by kibbutz members.

A kibbutz member named Charlie said, "In terms of respect there are three levels: The volunteers are the most respected... The Arabs have the second most respect... And the ulpanists are respected the third most."

Incidentally the volunteers were predominantly non-Jewish—and the ulpanists consisted mostly of Jewish men and women.

Charlie, who was a gentile, initially arrived at this kibbutz to work as a volunteer. He applied for membership—and was voted in by members. On Kibbutz Hukuk a Jewish woman had applied for membership and lost the vote. This was justified on the basis that there weren't enough similarly aged young men on that settlement.

Doug, who had also worked on an archaeological dig in Israel, told me that he knew of an Israeli who was born and brought up on a kibbutz being refused membership.

I had been told that the best kibbutzim to live on were the old ones. They were said to be wealthier than the young ones. I was informed that Kibbutz Haogen was the third richest... Each Member family possessed a car, telephone, video and bungalow-type accommodation. I had been given an account of life on a new kibbutz where its members lived in tents while they built the settlement... and toiling for more hours in a week than the eight hours a day members worked on Kibbutz Haogen.

After being on Kibbutz Haogen for a few months I used the several free days to which I was entitled to visit different places in Israel. I was accompanied by a Canadian student named Cecile.

We visited my old kibbutz—where I spoke with people I knew there before. The bar had become an unused waterlogged wreck.

Cecile was particularly interested in the nearby town of Sefat—because it was said to have a hundred art galleries. She spent hours looking at paintings.

We also went to an oasis like park in northern Israel.

After a swim in the clear natural water, I left her for several minutes.

On returning to the grassy area where she sat were seated four men. As I sat they politely introduced themselves. In conversation we were told that they were PLO members.

One of them said, "This park belongs to my grandfather... The Israelis took this park from him. We are now fighting to take it back!"

Another of them said that he studied in Bulgaria. He added, "I am a communist. The PLO is everywhere. I want to share this country with everyone... I'm not against the Israelis!"

Before leaving us, one of them invited her and me to join his family to eat with them in Nazareth.

We also visited Greg at his kibbutz in southern Israel. He hadn't yet met his guru.

Cecile and I visited Jerusalem.

She was both stubborn and direct while bartering with stall owners in the bazaars with their coffee aromas—where some old men smoked hubbly-bubbly pipes, and the odd spontaneous knife fight took place.

Cecile knocked down the price of a white dress from a thousand shekels to fifty.

I had been told that the Arab sellers charged American customers double what they made from other foreign nationalities... And they were able to differentiate between theirs and Canadian accents.

While in Jerusalem we stayed at Mr A's hostel. It had a run-down old character—whose quixotic atmosphere was magnified by the eccentric Mr A. He expelled people for whistling.

I found the old city of Jerusalem to be the cheapest place in Israel. Mr A's was situated in the Armenian quarter, and a night's stay was the same price as a standard bar of chocolate.

We visited the Holocaust Museum. Our visit was of a special importance for Cecile; we located in the museum's grounds a small tree—with Cecile's grandmother's name by it. It was placed as a tribute, along with other names by trees, to the gentiles who had helped the Jews during the Second World War. Cecile's family in Holland had hidden Jews in their home—away from the Nazis.

An aspect of Kibbutz life I particularly enjoyed was that we were taken on trips.

One trip I unintentionally met Burnley Mick, whom I had known in Greece. He told me in Jericho that The Top Ganger and his friends were all settled on Moshavim

During early June I left Israel.

A trip to Jericho

A few days after leaving Israel I visited Joe at the cottage he shared with his girlfriend at Tolo.

He had remained in Greece since the start of the oranges—and did various odd jobs once they had finished.

He very much enjoyed living in Greece—and had no intention of returning to work at Friday Bridge Camp.

I was offered factory and construction work in Greece... but I refused. I intended my next job to be working in the fishing industry in Iceland.

I was interested to know what had happened to Dutch Mike—once he had been arrested for breaking into a cafe.

Joe told me that Dutch Mike had implicated Toti—a four-foot ten scouser—even though he was innocent. Even though Dutch Mike said Toti was innocent, in court, the judge said it was too late. Both of them were jailed for seven months.

Toti was happy when Oggie and other cave dwellers were also jailed. They were jailed for thirty days.

Joe laughed as he continued, "They were supposed to be freed on a Monday... but asked to be freed on a Tuesday... On Tuesdays they had their favourite meal: hamburgers!"

They were all deported on release from jail.

I had known Oggie at Friday Bridge Camp. While in Greece I was told that he was travelling on a friend's passport.

Toti had become depressed once his friends were released. After ten weeks in prison he was released. He had sent home for money—and paid four hundred pounds to buy himself from out of prison.

CHAPTER NINE

DURING THE EARLY PART of July, 1983, I returned to Friday Bridge Camp—due to the plans I had made regarding employment in the Icelandic fishing industry having failed.

Soon after I had arrived on the camp I was told there had been a battle with locals. Locals had, on the previous night, attacked campers, with an array of weapons.

One camper had been sitting with his girlfriend on an outside bench; he received paralysis after being hit by metallic objects.

The police took locals and campers away for questioning. Courgette gangers Big Al and Big Jim, who had used violence against locals, were later released without charge.

During my first day of the new season, detectives assembled an inquiry in the writing room. Even though The Top Ganger hadn't been involved in the previous night's violence, he tried to lead the investigation. Consequently a detective told him to be seated and be quiet.

Some of the locals received prison sentences for their parts in the attack.

Subsequently the camp became like a prison: uniformed men leading Alsatians patrolled the camp during the evenings.

I had no intentions of being a courgette ganger again; I just wanted to be a cutter.

Once I arrived on the courgette fields I saw Gus, the German foreman, scrutinize the workers.

He said to me, "You were here last year... so you'll be a ganger."

I retorted, "I don't want to be a ganger! I just wanted to be a cutter until I can find a better seasonal job."

Gus barked back, "You know the job!"

Consequently I took a gang to the vegetables.

Due to there being comparatively more work on the courgettes, overall, than on other crops, veterans like John the Cowboy, who didn't usually work for this company, found themselves working on the courgettes. John the Cowboy worked in the loading gang with Charlie. Charlie was fifty and stout, having a mop of blond hair.

During a misty morning, Charlie said to John, "Keep watch while I go out there."

Charlie took cabbages from the rows' centres—believing that no-one would notice the theft—as if it had happened at the start of the rows.

On returning to the van Charlie justified his actions: "Everyone steals... don't they? No one's honest!"

Later, the Cowboy said of Charlie, "He be a pure gypsy. I wouldn't trust him an inch!"

Charlie deliberately made problems for the gangers. He readily informed on them, to Gus. The gangers set traps in order to find out the informer under determination; eventually Charlie was revealed as the person who had been exposing their fiddles, to Gus. Charlie caused trouble for them—so that attention was removed from him, allowing himself and John to enjoy coffee and cake at his caravan during parts of afternoons.

I decided to resign from my ganger's job: I and a man whom I have decided to name 'The Nonentity Ganger' were given each two workers less than the other gangers; and, at the end of a working day, Gus discovered that we were unable to cover the same amount of acreage as the others. Consequently he spoke about sacking the two of us; but a decision would be taken once the courgette boss had returned from holiday.

I said to the other gangers that I was leaving the camp—and would return for the plum season.

The Top Ganger tried to stop me from leaving, explaining that the courgette boss would make sure that we weren't sacked.

I explained that I wouldn't work under Gus again. If my boss is ruthless, I will accept his or her leadership, providing that he or she understands the work... But when a boss is harsh and professionally incompetent, this I will not suffer. I added that I didn't like the courgette boss—and envisaged that conditions would become worse for the gangers.

I returned to Friday Bridge Camp to find that I was allocated work on the plum harvest. I had been told that the labour officer read every postcard that arrived at the camp office—so I sent several postcards to the camp saying I would be there for the plums.

Andy told me that on receiving my postcard, the Labour Officer had joked to him, "I see John wants to work on the courgettes."

I found out that The Nonentity Ganger hadn't been sacked; the courgette boss, on returning from holiday, accepted that Gus had been wrong in wanting to relieve us of our gangs.

I worked on the plums—for Ayres—at Elm. One of the workers that I knew before was a fireman known as Dick the Walker—who was near retirement age. I had shared a hut with him in 1980. Dick was like me in the respect that he had transferred to the plums, due to grievances against the courgette company. While younger campers would relax after work, Dick used to sometimes take a ten-mile stroll about the Fenland.

Also working with me was a professional darts player from Liverpool. Being aged in his thirties, he bellyached to me, "I was picking apples at Woodrow's on an hourly rate... and his wife watched me slog my guts out all afternoon. When we were getting paid I expected more money... but I was paid at the same rate!"

What I concede Woodrow's girlfriend, not wife, was thinking, is—what a mug! I'll ask the labour officer to send a dozen more campers like this one! When an employer, as in the darts player's case, says that a day's wage is twelve pounds, then that's what it means; unless one doesn't do enough work!

Ayres was concerned that he might lose some of his apple crop through gale damage, so he indicated that he would pay us more if we prematurely picked an exposed section—but at the end of this work the payment of twelve pounds remained unchallenged.

The professional darts player bellyached in a quiet tone, "Someone should tell him... someone should tell him!"

But I didn't mind working for Ayres: he always paid his workers at the legal day rate; and there wasn't the cruelty that I had known in some other workplaces; we were able to have a laugh at Ayres.

The cordial working experiences I knew at Ayres were dissimilar from those of my former colleagues on the courgette fields. They complained about the aggravation that they received from Gus and the courgette boss.

The courgette boss who had become the Chairman of Friday Bridge Camp ordered the labour officer to send Big AI, Big Jim, Little Al and The Nonentity Ganger to work for Roy the Ganger at the process factory, for four days. The courgette boss justified why they had been sent to work for the worst Friday Bridge employer by saying that he wanted them to appreciate how fortunate they were... to be able to work for him.

During an evening the courgette boss took The Top Ganger, his girlfriend and The Proverbial Monetary Socialist out to dinner.

Before leaving the camp in September I conceded that the courgette boss didn't know his workers well enough: his best ganger was Big Al... and the most insidious ganger was taken to dinner.

CHAPTER TEN

DURING THE MIDDLE of September I arrived at a farm in Kent to harvest apples, finding myself to be the first of the seasonal workers there. As the day progressed I was joined in the shack by Brian, Paul and a courting couple.

As the days passed by I found the atmosphere to be antagonistic: Paul, being an agricultural student from Oxford, moaned because I had a room to myself—while he had to share a room with Brian. Brian protested that the squeaky noises Paul made at night kept him awake. Paul forcefully stated that we should share in meals, adding that it was stupid for anyone to buy food just for oneself.

I chose to pay for my own nutritional requirements since there aren't many types of food that I like; for example, the only type of eggs I will eat must be made of chocolate!

Eventually, it was decided that we took turns to make porridge.

I found Brian to be a most inconsistent man: one evening he was English—on another night he was Welsh; Brian said that he didn't believe in God—yet maintained that it was impossible not for ghosts to exist; he proudly espoused socialism—whilst alternatively telling us of his capitalist aspirations. Brian was the best apple picker on Westerhill Farm: he picked more fruit of a better quality than the rest of us did; but he complained that we didn't give him any credit. Brian couldn't stand us talking about better apple pickers than him; he either changed the conversation or justified himself, saying that the only reason anyone could pick more apples than he was because that person didn't do the job properly; Brian said this of the apple pickers he worked with in Australia who picked several bins a day more than him. He added that the picking in Australia was much rougher than in Kent, and the apple pickers in Victoria wouldn't last long at Westerhill Farm—due to our fussy employer and his stringent working conditions. Brian laughed as he continued, "They would wreck this orchard. There would be broken branches all over the place."

During a working day, someone picked the same amount as Brian and he started making excuses for this emulation.

Brian, being big, dark and hairy, was highly critical and hypersensitive to receiving criticism. He said that my hairy head resembled a coconut—and that my nose was like a Roman's.

The impression that I picked up from Brian was that if he had worked for a month tomato picking for my farmer on Moshav Hatzeva, it would have damaged his back—and broken his heart.

The male part of the courting couple admitted that he was wanted by the police. He was proud of his fast-handed girlfriend who used her speed to steal goods each week from Maidstone. He boasted a pair of trainers to us… which she had purloined.

Some evenings we sat about the fire giving factual accounts of ourselves while eating supper.

The male part of the courting couple said, "I was working in a shoe repair shop where people paid me a pound deposit, but I used to pocket some of the deposits. One day a woman came in and gave me a pound note... and, after-she left, I put it in my pocket. Fifteen minutes later the woman returned and asked me to empty my pocket. In my pocket was her pound note that she had previously marked! I lost my job. The firm must have been suspicious. The job was good and paid well, but I wanted to go out that night.

Brian and I had watched him cheat at cards at The Bull in Linton. One night he drunkenly boasted, after returning from a pub, "I'm fifteen quid better off than when I went out. I won it at cards."

On another evening he returned from a pub—and told us that locals had told him that they were being paid seven pounds a bin, while we were receiving three pounds twenty-five per bin.

Our ganger told us that our rate of pay was the same as that in 1982. She seemed to be resentful of us. I believed that this was because we earned more than her—because she was on a set gangers rate while we were on piece rate.

Due to thefts of food a bad atmosphere was created, where different members of our abode stopped speaking to certain individuals.

Brian was my only friend at Westerhill Farm. We went drinking at pubs in Maidstone, Linton, Marden and Coxheath. I found Brian to be interesting. He had spent nearly fifteen years working in Australia. I was amazed by the amounts of fruit Brian told me that some people picked in Victoria: the top pickers picked sixteen bins a day; but some had harvested twenty bins in a day, and an Indian had picked twenty-three bins in a day.

At the end of the season I was asked by the farmer's son to return for the 1984 harvest.

Although I considered a wage of between sixteen and thirty pounds a day to be good, I felt that my employers wanted too much for too little because the bin rates were low—on the strictest farm that I had worked for, even though we had a free place to live.

CHAPTER ELEVEN

DURING THE LATE NOVEMBER of 1983 I arrived at the Festos hostel in Athens.

On finding that I was to share a mixed sex dormitory, the idea of having an alcoholic drink occurred to me to help me sleep. I went to the hostel's bar—to find Charlie and Julie serving. I had known them in Nafplion. There was a sense of surprise from both sides of the bar.

I gave Julie a hundred drachma note for a drink. She gave me an ouzo plus two fifty drachma notes.

In conversation, they said that they were working at Festos until the oranges started; and, that they would meet me in Nafplion. I told them I was going to a town further south than Nafplion—for this season.

After leaving Athens I went to Nafplion... in anticipation of a day's visit. Soon after I had booked into a hotel in the town's periphery, I walked into central Nafplion.

While sitting outside Haries Cafe I was surprised to see John the Cowboy and Steve from Stockport walking towards me. I was particularly surprised to see John—seeing that this was the first time he had left the British Isles—even though he had been involved in seasonal work since the fifties.

The three of us entered Haries for a drink. Whilst inside the café they told me that there was no work.

I told them that I was heading south during the next day. As we continued to drink I noticed that other drinkers were depressed—due to the prospect of being unemployed.

Suddenly the door opened and we watched a Greek enter. He walked to me, shook my hand, and said, "How are you, John?" Once I replied Barri continued, "Could you get me fifteen people? We work tomorrow."

As I continued to talk with the tall afro-haired man, an Irish voice bellowed, "See that man, (referring to me) I worked with him for eight years… on the courgettes."

Barri looked confusedly at John the Cowboy.

During the past season I had brought waterproofs but hadn't found much need for them—but I made a mistake in not bringing them a year later due to the heavy rain. We tolerated picking oranges for four days whilst wearing rain saturated clothes—due to there being so little work available.

Suddenly, our work was terminated due to our agent Zachariki being jailed for employing illegal workers. Consequently Barri was unable to pay us; but some of his workers thought he was trying to purloin their wages. Fortunately he managed to convince the poverty-stricken mob that was about to attack him that he could not pay them until his agent had been released from prison.

On returning to my hotel I saw Jiame smiling at me in the corridor. We shook hands while exchanging greetings.

We subsequently visited various bars. In one he asked me to choose a gang—for orange picking.

While in town I saw the courting couple I worked with in Kent. I didn't make contact with them: if I dislike people in one country, I will be impartial to them in another!

Eventually most of Jiame's gang was made up of people I had known before—such as people who had worked at Friday Bridge like Joe and Ken.

Joe who used to work in the cookhouse at Friday Bridge Camp said to me, "This would be a good-looking gang... if you weren't in it!"

But it was John the Cowboy who was regarded as the gang's comedian. Sometimes he became drunk at work—and due to him drinking too much retsina he became lost in orchards when doing ladder work, picking the top fruit that the rest of us had left.

Another couple of gang members had taken six weeks—cycling from Kent to Greece—after finishing doing seasonal work in Marden.

An eccentric gang member called Vondarge Pete differed from most of us in the respect that he was cultured. Being a former history undergraduate, he gave me the impression that he wanted to rid himself of a good family life and get lost in various seasonal work circuits. Pete had travelled about the Middle East and through popular culture routes in Asia.

A gang member whom I hadn't worked with before was a Kiwi named Rozane, who was Jiame's girlfriend. We became friends, and through Rozane I was introduced to Kerry, her sister, who worked at an hotel.

During days in which I didn't work I visited Kerry in the hotel's reception where she read my hand palms.

She predicted that I would be successful.

I told various people about my palm reading. They asked me to remember them. Years later—I have remembered—I have remembered to forget them.

The oranges at Nafplion

The hotel that I stayed in wasn't as good as the Acropal Hotel. It was fairly rundown—and run in an undisciplined way. My sink had become blocked—in the room which I occupied alone. Consequently I asked the hotel owner to unblock it. I found him to be a young, smarmy man who regularly said in an insincere way on seeing me: "Yasso, Yanni!"

He gave me a plunger to empty the dirt saturated water, but it did little good.

One day I returned from work and found that my room had been impressively cleaned. The empty sink shined. During this day I was asked to move to another room. This was because a Greek guest was to replace me, whereas the other guests were foreigners who shared rooms.

I was moved in with a middle-aged Irishman named Mick. The hotel owner said to me, "I charge you less… he is a tourist."

Due to there being days when I was unable to work I slept in. During such a morning, when Mick was out, the door crashed open. A bent figure entered with a mop and bucket. It was Mad Annie. After asking me for some money she inverted some of Mick's shampoo to the deck, added some water and began mopping the floor.

Mad Annie was a well-known, bent-backed local woman who was sometimes found hiding behind doors—whilst imbibing wine. She regularly demanded money, coffee or retsina, on seeing me. I took advantage of her having a bad back: I hid my cooking utensils under the bed, a spot that was out of her reach. I used this tactic after finding my cooking gear on the steps outside my room. She had, without asking me, used this equipment to make coffee for some of the other guests, which she charged them for.

During the latter part of January 1984 the possibility of finding work became so difficult that I decided to visit

Turkey rather than sit idly in bars and cafés waiting for employment. Jiame's gang had during this period disbanded.

I asked John the Cowboy if he wanted to join me in a visit to Turkey. He said that he wanted to go—but I hadn't given him enough notice.

I sat in a carriage on the Istanbul-bound train.

A woman who sat opposite me expressed enthusiastically in a Surrey voice, on seeing that my belongings were kept in a plastic bag, "I'm impressed!"

I thought: "How can anyone be impressed by impoverishment?" Nevertheless there were those culture-vulture budget travellers that were impressed by poverty. Whether these states of poverty were authentically or intentionally experienced seemed to me to be immaterial... to them.

The young Surrey woman subsequently discussed the Copious Luteum and relatable topics with her companions— obliging me to vacate from their bloody conversation!

At the border point a large man entered the compartment where I sat alone.

He said, "Luggage?"

I showed him my bag.

He softly returned, "No problem."

He then forcefully disassembled the seats and apparently, from out of nowhere, a small transparent packet with a white substance showing through it appeared on a seat.

Fast thoughts entered my brain. I was thinking that someone had planted drugs on me. I was almost panicking as

I looked at the packet while contemplating whether to throw it through the window.

The immigration officer nonchalantly viewed the packet—before chucking it through the window! He then reassembled the seats. The immigration officer twice returned—and kindly, on both occasions, gave me nuts.

Before arriving in Istanbul a conductor asked me if I wanted to change currency. I declined on the grounds that I anticipated being able to obtain better exchange rates in Istanbul.

After going to various parts of Istanbul, I visited the Pudding Shop.

Even though there were uniformed police within, a scruffy man in a long coat whispered to me, "Hashish, hashish?"

Soon after the pusher left a man sat down opposite me at my table.

After several minutes of talking, he offered me a job: smuggling illegal immigrants into Greece. There were to be six of us—with myself being the only member that wasn't a Pakistani. I refused.

After leaving the Pudding Shop I contemplated visiting other places in Turkey on my way back to Greece.

I had regretted not exchanging money on the train. I found it very difficult to change drachmas into lire; none of the banks I went to in Istanbul would change it. Eventually I found a private dealer who exchanged it—at a very bad rate.

I caught the Athens-bound train and disembarked on the Turkish border town at Uzunkoprü—to experience the early morning coldness in a dark environment.

I subsequently relished some comfort in the railway café, sitting by the fire drinking glasses of chi.

Due to the café boss learning that I was neither Turkish nor Greek he refused to accept payment for the several glasses of the warm brown fluid which I had consumed.

I left the café and encountered the dawn coldness—a biting coldness that I hadn't felt previously, which seemed to match with the bleak scenery.

I took a train journey to Apullo.

As I walked about Apullo I saw gangs of workmen giving me the impression that this was a hardworking area.

I visited a café for a dish of soup.

In conversation with the cook I told him that I was a tourist. Consequently he twice rushed to fill my bowl, and refused to take payment.

After my meal I decided to go to Pehlivankoy.

On arriving at the train under determination the driver asked me where I wanted to go to. Once I told him where he invited me to climb into the driver's compartment.

I spent the journey—drinking chi—whilst being involved in some light conversation and joking with the driver and a couple of other railway staff.

At the Pehlivankoy station, the inspector said something in a perplexed state, on seeing me leave the compartment.

I then visited a bar where I found the bottled lager to hold a chemical taste. I sipped this for most of the afternoon while becoming friendly with the owner and his staff. They refused to accept any payment from me; but, on noticing that I had become drunk, the owner's son escorted me to an hotel.

A policeman at the hotel aggressively wanted to know my identity; then demanded that I was only to stay for one night in this town!

After spending a few hours asleep someone banged and shouted at my door.

I opened the door to see the hotel manager; behind him, sitting on a bench, sat a meditating man. The hotel manager asked me to follow him.

We went outside—then returned to the bar.

The owner's son had prepared a feast for me. I was treated like a celebrity... shaking hands with everyone present. So much kindness was shown to me—yet the only thing that the owner's son asked from me was for me to send him a postcard.

The owner's son said, "We are kind... because we have little money... so money isn't a problem. The Greeks are greedy. Money is a problem for them—they have money!"

I found that there was an overt dislike for both Arabs and Greeks in this area.

The cafe owner's son warned me about the dangers of being seen outside late at night by the police. He had been beaten by the police, after defying the curfew.

After my meal the cafe owner's son took me to the train station. He bought me a ticket, then said farewell.

After arriving at Uzunkoprü I visited another bar; I found that some of the customers already knew my name.

A man recorded each bottle of lager I drank. While drinking I became aware that I was the only person in the full café that consumed this type of alcohol.

One of the customers bought me a snack—then warned me not to be seen outside late by the police.

I later took his advice—then slept in a railway waiting room where a fire blazed.

I returned to Nafplion to find that the work was re-starting. I was invited to join a gang that was headed by Big Al, Alci Alan, Big Jim and Portuguese Jorge. It was composed of the remainders of disbanded gangs, predominantly.

Three of this gang's leaders I had known at Friday Bridge Camp: but, what was unusual about this outfit was that the four gangers paid themselves the same rate as the workers.

I liked Alci Alan who I hadn't worked with before. He impressed me in perceiving that he held a high academic potential—which was accompanied by a good nature. Alci Alan told me he once arrived on a Greek Island with only one drachma—but, soon after going there, he found a job selling photographs to tourists.

He had sacked one gang member for calling him a drunken bum.

Another gang member—and friend of his—returned, "But Al... you *are* a drunken bum!"

Alci Alan replied, "I know... but he didn't have to tell me!"

There was a physically beautiful Brazilian seasonal worker known as Miss World—who so many men in town were trying to seduce. Alci Alan, being of a wild appearance (showing missing front teeth) had a sexual relationship with this South American beauty, whereas the likes of Portuguese Jorge were rejected! Jorge wouldn't accept her rejection—justifying himself by saying that he had been rejected because she wasn't heterosexual.

After several days this gang disbanded.

I managed to find work on a building site, but after spending several days mixing cement I lost the partial use of both my hands—and black holes were sporadically situated on my fingers. Consequently I was unable to work.

Some other seasonal workers had found employment in construction; for example, after doing the orange season, Ken did building work before returning to Friday Bridge Camp.

Before leaving Greece I read in a newspaper that six Pakistanis had been caught illegally entering Greece from Turkey. I still wonder whether it was the outfit I had been asked to join, in the Pudding Shop?

I left Greece towards the end of February.

CHAPTER TWELVE

DURING JUNE 1984 I arrived in the latter part of the afternoon at Newtown Farm, Gloucestershire.

The farm owner asked me to start work during the evening of my arrival day. I worked with two men named Kendo and Paul clearing out old lettuce leaves from within a plastic tunnel.

I was impressed by the well-organized and favourable working conditions—which were in accordance with the considerate accommodation.

Having a real bed in a room of my own—plus the availability of a bath, very good cooking facilities and a well-furnished sitting room—made me realize how fortunate I was to work there.

Whereas at Westerhill Farm part of the seating arrangement involved sitting on apple boxes, at Newtown Farm we had unbroken chairs and a comfortable settee to use.

The good paying employment in ordered working systems, as at Newtown Farm, was what I had longed for.

The boss was said to own three farms; one being Ploddy House. This farm was once known as Bloody House due to someone being murdered there.

The regular staff consisted of a friendly crew being headed by two managers: Graham and Roger. Graham was in charge of the lettuce; while Roger controlled the potato, runner bean and sugarbeet harvests.

The person who was directly in charge of me was named Kevin. Kevin tried to conceal from us that he was a foreman—and worked with us as if he had been an ordinary worker. His mad personality created a funny working environment.

We often went to the village of Newent to visit the pubs—where I found the locals to be more friendly than those in the Wisbech area.

I found Kendo—a Brummie—to be an unusual man: he was obsessed in paying for our drinks and meals. Even when he wasn't drinking with us, Kendo suddenly appeared in our local, bought us all a drink, then left.

After last orders we went to the chip van. Kendo reappeared and pleaded with us to allow him to pay for our meals.

Every Saturday morning a debt collector arrived—looking for Kendo, and somehow he couldn't be found—to repay the thousands of pounds that he had borrowed from a loan company.

While I was contented to earn between one hundred and ten and one hundred and twenty pounds a week, Kendo earned considerably more—due to him working more hours than the rest of us did.

Kendo sent his girlfriend fifty pounds a week. He fondly told me that she relished consuming twenty pound bottles of champagne.

One weekend he visited her in Birmingham. At 11 o'clock—after he spent the best part of two hundred pounds—she told him to leave her home because she expected the arrival of her boyfriend.

An emotionally devastated Kendo stopped sending money to her. A few weeks later she wrote to him asking if he would be prepared to resume their relationship.

During my seventh week in Gloucestershire I resigned from my job at Newtown Farm.

CHAPTER THIRTEEN

ON LEAVING GLOUCESTERSHIRE I made my way to East Anglia—arriving there during an August evening.

I was told that Old George the hunch-backed gardener had died.

He was the only long time staff member that I hadn't spoken with. This was because I wasn't important enough—for him to converse with me. When drinking in the club George refused to be served by anyone other than the head barman. George, I believe, loved life on the camp; and I know that he told another staff member who complained about the conditions "to fuck off…and leave!"

Another staff member who no longer worked on the camp was the middle-aged Pole known as Big John. I had heard him suggest in conversation that he was too important to be sacked. Big John was no longer at the camp—because he had been sacked.

Andy, whom I had known since 1980, had lost his ganger's position. The labour officer had stopped giving him work. Consequently Andy managed to find work on an external farm. The labour officer found out that Andy had been finding his own work—hence he ordered him to leave the camp.

My immunity from working on the courgettes hadn't been removed. I was allocated work at Ayres.

On arrival at the farm in question I was the last to leave the van.

I watched the farm workers named Dick and Ron chat in a humorous way on seeing me.

After welcoming me, Dick asked me to be in charge of the pickers on the plum harvest.

I liked working with Dick, Ron and another regular worker named Brian because they enjoyed joking with the campers.

One camper that made us laugh was a middle-aged, bespectacled scouser named Tio. The loudness of his voice was often heard disrupting various subjects of conversation.

On taking his fruit to be weighed he asked, "How many have I picked?"

"Four boxes," replied Ron.

Tio retorted, "You're robbing me… I've done six!"

Ron laughed.

We worked on the plums, along with didicoys, who worked on a separate section. Eventually, we worked on the same rows. As they worked from the opposite ends, they put a teenaged girl to work a few trees ahead of us—expecting my gang to stop on reaching her.

Dick shouted to me, "Send them in!"

The Algerians and Moroccans jumped like pirates invading a ship as they swung through the trees of the didicoys.

A didicoy named Nelson told me about the discrimination he had suffered at a pub at Elm. "I went for the first time to the Bell for a drink, and I was wearing a suit and I had never seen the landlord before… and he refused to serve me." He was refused service because he was suspected of being a vandweller.

Tio died at Friday Bridge Camp. One morning he awoke, after spending the previous night heavily consuming beer. He went to wash his socks, then returned to his bed—to die.

I was told that during the season of Tio's death his daughter had gone to the camp and asked her father if he wanted his estranged wife back. He responded, "Want her back? I don't want her front, let alone her back!"

I left Friday Bridge Camp at the end of August.

The Fenland

CHAPTER FOURTEEN

I **RETURNED TO FRIDAY BRIDGE CAMP** in the July of 1985 with my sister Julia. On seeing us, the labour officer and his wife welcomed us. They remembered Julia from 1982 when she had spent a holiday on the camp.

Due to the labour officer seeing me dressed in a suit, he responded, "I sense a con!"

I spent part of the first week of this season harvesting strawberries. At the end of this week I bade my sister farewell.

Before seeing my sister off, Japanese John approached me in a suspicious way, then said that the labour officer wanted to see me.

On arrival at the office, the labour officer asked me if I wanted to work in the kitchen—and on security; he stressed that the latter form of employment wasn't a punch-up job.

I accepted. I was then told by the labour officer to report to Steve in the kitchen.

On arrival in the cookhouse I said to the elderly Ukrainian man who had recently been put in charge of cooking due to old Polish Bodna having died, "I've been sent to work here."

Steve responded, "You crazy bastard... shit on the floor!"

It was an odd thing to say since there was enough muck on the deck to justify the construction of a miniature mud hut.

Both Steve and Bodna had been prisoners of war in East Anglia—yet had spent most of their lives as free men living all year round on Friday Bridge Camp, working from Spring until October on it.

Apart from Steve and the breakfast cook, the other members of the catering team hadn't been going to the camp as long as me. One of them, a Welshman, said that he and a Jersey man named Andy, and Steve from Stockport, were at war with the chins. Blodwyn explained that the name 'Chin' was the nickname of the gangers—adding that their chins grew when they couldn't have their own ways. Andy said that when he went into the dining room, The Top Ganger's chin was stuck in his custard.

Steve from Stockport, who worked as a van driver, said that he, Andy, and Blodwyn had been in a conflagration with the gangers at the Bridge. While drinking in this pub The Top Ganger approached them and demanded to know why the three of them wouldn't join his clique, explaining that it was the done thing for the kitchen boys and the gangers to go around as one gang.

Andy told him that they weren't interested.

The Top Ganger retorted that they should give them more food, like Joe and Mick had previously done.

Andy had said that they would receive the same quantities of food as the other campers. He added that he wouldn't socialize with the gangers because he found The Top Ganger to be a bore. Subsequently Japanese John prevented the two groups—whose members were aged from between their late teens until their early forties—from fighting.

On leaving the Bridge the two groups shouted insults as they walked to the camp.

The main cause of anger, regarding the courgette gangers, was that during the planting, in May, they received sixteen pounds a day plus sixteen pounds a week each for ganging, but once the cutting had begun their earnings were changed to twelve pounds a day plus twelve pounds a week for ganging.

Yet vandwellers who had been planting alongside the courgette gangers had been paid twenty-five pounds a day. Once the cutting started, their wages were dropped to twenty pounds a day; but they refused to work for this amount—so they finished working for the courgette company.

The Top Ganger said to me that when there were sixty-seven acres of courgettes, sixty-two acres were as profit; but, in 1985 the courgette acreage was more than one hundred. Yet The Top Ganger and his girlfriend had less to complain about than the other gangers since they were the only two campers that were given free accommodation.

I was employed in the catering department on a part-time basis; the remainder of my working week was spent doing security and agricultural work.

The breakfast cook was in charge of me during the morning shift. I was surprised that he had survived as a staff member since 1980. Whenever one of the junior catering members wanted to use a toilet, the breakfast cook asked,

"What are you going to do, piss or shit?" Whatever the answer, he made a time check.

The breakfast chef regularly reprimanded part-time workers. One in particular seemed to me to possess a magic mushroom induced consciousness. His face told me that his grandfather had been kind to him; no matter what trick the elderly man played on him there would always be a happy end product.

One of my old friends, John the Yank, also worked as a part-time kitchen worker. John had spent 1981, 1982, and 1983 working as a dishwasher in a German hotel; and had returned to the camp in 1984 after leaving it in 1980. He had been a staff sergeant in the US army—but had become invalided out of it due to losing an eye. He had subsequently worked in Australia for six years.

The main complaint about John, in the kitchen, was that the ash from the Senior Service cigarettes he smoked while dishwashing landed on the crockery.

There was a lot of conflict between the catering staff and campers—due to the meagre, low quality food we served.

An army-trained cook named John, who was recently employed in the catering department, said to the campers who complained about their dreadful meals, "Bad food can't be made good... no matter what is done to it!"

The breakfast cook responded differently from John's approach. He said, "I have only two words to tell complaining campers... and that's—Fuck off!"

I watched the breakfast cook try to smash a pile of plates on the head of a complaining Algerian camper.

Andy was threatened with the sack by the labour officer for pulling a complaining camper over the food counter.

The only person in the kitchen that I felt didn't like me was the courgette boss, who was, as well as being the chairman, the head of catering. He said good morning to everyone except me on arrival in the cooking area.

John the Cowboy tried to use his friendship with me—so that he could receive large food portions. One morning as I served him cornflakes he emphatically pleaded, "More, more—pile it on!"

A slow threatening voice seethed from behind me, "I'm watching you!" I turned to see the breakfast cook.

I returned—to the direction of my vision—to watch John slam his hands on the counter. He sharply returned, "And I'm watching you!"

John the Yank didn't work for the whole season in the cookhouse: he, John the Cowboy and I went to the Peterborough Cowboy and Western Show during a Saturday morning. John, being scheduled to work on the afternoon shift, decided to stay in Peterborough. On returning to the camp, he was sacked. Consequently John the Yank returned to work in the fields and factories on a full-time basis.

John differed from the middle-aged and elderly heterosexual celibates at the camp, who regarded an adult life of staying single as an achievement. He wanted a second wife after an unsuccessful marriage in Germany. Although John was a charming, heavy smoking, hard drinking romantic, he had very few material assets—and had little more than memories to relate to those that were prepared to listen.

John the Yank is now a memory: he died, aged fifty, in 1990.

During the 1985 season I lived in the geriatrics section... since it was usually quieter than the other places used by young campers, and it was close to the cookhouse.

One morning I was lying in my sleeping place anticipating my shift to begin when I heard an explosion in the cookhouse.

I rushed to the cooking area to see utensils on the deck.

The breakfast cook held a hand shouting, "I've burnt all the hairs on my hand! I have spent six years in the army and twenty-seven at sea and never have I been with such idiots!"

His comments referred to the staff member who had left the gas on from the previous shift; subsequently, the breakfast cook, being an alcoholic, had arrived to light the oven, partly drunk.

I regarded the breakfast cook to have been a decent person—whose good qualities had become tarnished due to his dependency on alcohol. He owed so much money to campers, staff members and locals. His deathly yellow face was stretched on its bones. He drank alcohol throughout the day, starting in the early hours on vodka and whiskey... through his shift until he was able to drink beer in the club.

The breakfast cook had been using vile language as he drank at The Chequers. Consequently Hughie the landlord cautioned him on his choice of words. The breakfast cook obliged. Subsequently other drinkers started swearing— whom Hughie, being a former Fenland boxing champion, didn't try to stop.

The breakfast chef said to him, "Why don't you tell them to stop swearing?"

Hughie replied, "Oh… but… they are locals!"

The breakfast cook raged, "Locals… stuff your fucking beer!"

The breakfast cook died in 1989.

One of the people he used to borrow money from was a fifty-year old Glaswegian named Karl.

Karl was a person that no-one at the camp made trouble for. Being a former forester he used his sledgehammer like fists, on occasions, to sort out people with conflicting interests from his. When plum picking Karl punched an Italian camper he found taking his fruit.

On arriving at a factory, a young local man made fun of Karl as he entered the building. The Scotsman punched him.

Consequently the bloody faced local shouted, "I'll get my father and uncle!"

Karl retorted, "Get the whole factory."

Karl remained at the camp for six months of each season before going to live in Wisbech… then worked on the winter crops. He told me that there was plenty of well-paid work in Holbeach during the cold months.

Karl was in the same situation as me, in respect that he was exempt from working for the courgette boss. He worked mostly for Roy the ganger.

I had observed Roy the ganger's unpleasant character to be commensurable with his appearance. His regular gang of workers consisted predominantly of locals—who spoke in abnormally pitched voices—and had mildly Neanderthal facial features, giving me the impression that they were the products of the mechanism of fenland incest. Roy and his gang were banned from the camp's clubhouse—for causing trouble.

Roy the ganger had paid the campers with the exception of Karl, at the same rate for several years—and depended on child labour whose wages were even less than what the campers earned. Karl was paid at a higher rate than the rest of the campers were.

A local woman was perturbed by Roy the ganger's behaviour. She said to me that he had approached her! Then he said, "If I was a man I'd fuck you."

Some young local women at a factory asked Karl as he entered the building, "How's your balls?"

Giving them a Scottish chuckle he replied, "They're alright."

The Top Ganger knew more about Roy the ganger than any of the other campers. He had worked with him in 1979—when Roy was the ganger of the courgettes.

The Top Ganger said to me regarding Roy, "He was ruthless… sending campers back to the camp for missing one courgette… They were being sent back all the time… until he was sacked."

He was dismissed for conning the courgette boss. The Top Ganger explained, "If Roy wanted a dozen workers… out on the courgette fields… he asked for twenty, using the extra workers to do other jobs so he was paid twice for them."

The Top Ganger told me that he had done private work for Roy in 1979. His earnings were more, then, than what campers were paid by Roy in 1985.

The Top Ganger held a partial admiration for Roy the ganger, saying, "For someone who isn't from this area... who is a pig's ear... and Jewish... to do as well as he's done."

The security work that I was employed to do I did with Glasgow Jim and our superior—the head barman. The head barman was one of the most senior staff members to work on the camp. The head barman had been working at Friday Bridge Camp since 1960. Although he was an accomplished land worker, rarely was agricultural employment done by him. During the early stages of his adulthood he ventured, after each season at the camp, to work on the fishing vessels in Iceland.

The head barman told me of his experiences as a land worker at the camp in 1960, aged seventeen: "I worked for the first time in the PJ-Mick Cullen potato gang. I cried at the end of the first day it was so hard!" We earned six pounds a day—and a week's rent was five pounds. In those days there was plenty of work. There were a hundred acres of fruit. He laughed regarding newcomers to seasonal landwork, adding, "Fitness fanatics run about the camp on their first day. They work until Wednesday... then the magnetic bed stops them going out to work."

The head barman was devoted to the camp—and was against campers and staff members from consuming alcohol in local public houses, believing they should drink in the camp club. I noticed that he tended to befriend heavy drinkers—and became concerned if they were under employed, consequently sometimes using his influence to persuade the labour officer to give them regular work.

The head barman had no sympathy regarding the daily complaints made by the courgette gangers. He reckoned that they were underworked and overpaid people who didn't spend enough money in the club. He had tried with the head woman (his girlfriend) to be put in charge of the camp in 1983—when most of the directors wanted to get rid of the labour officer for a second time—because of the violence that had happened then. The labour officer wasn't removed because the courgette boss dissuaded the directors from doing so.

The labour officer was dismissed in the late seventies— but returned after a season's absence—because no-one suitable could be found to do his job.

Ken said that the person who took over the camp's management was a good man but left after one season because no-one would help him. The regular staff members wanted the labour officer to return.

The labour officer didn't care how much a camper spent in the club; his favouritism was based on whether or not he liked a person. No camper, irrespective of whether or not they received preferential treatment, could expect immunity from his wrath.

I was aware of the labour officer joking with a camper during a morning of the same day he ordered that person to leave the camp—in the afternoon.

Such treatment was allocated irrespective of whether it was a person's first or thirtieth season. This treatment was used often for the most trivial of reasons.

One camper who had been shown favouritism by the labour officer was nicknamed Stinky. Stinky, being big, bespectacled and having a mop of grey hair, liked being called this because it sounded posh!

The labour officer had offered him a special job, then changed his mind, claiming that he hadn't shown enough enthusiasm.

Stinky, aged forty-eight, used to go to bed in the same clothes that he worked and socialized in—muddy boots as well.

Some campers used to throw their leftover food on his bed—which he later devoured.

The labour officer ordered that he showered. Stinky, being fully clothed, stood under the water. Consequently, the gushing liquid forced out the lenses of his glasses.

Stinky had been drinking with an Australian camper known as the Robin Hood of March who bought him lagers and whiskies. Consequently, Stinky became so drunk that he lost his false teeth and glasses. He tried to find them by searching dustbins! His teeth were found near to a dyke. During the next day he went to work for Roy the ganger— and vomited at the production line.

The Robin Hood of March was so named because, after becoming drunk, he robbed a shop—after which he took the confectionary he had stolen to an old people's home—in March. Aged in his thirties, he was fined one hundred pounds for breaking into this shop in March.

Stinky was regarded as a good worker: some striking Nottingham coal miners who worked at the camp in 1984 said that he was the best worker they had ever seen. Yet he was among the lowest paid campers at Friday Bridge—due to him working regularly at the factories. Stinky had become fed up with hearing other campers talk about the comparably good wages they made on the apple crop—which he couldn't get a transfer to. Consequently Stinky found a private job earning good money on the apples at Wisbech St Marys.

One morning Stinky and another camper were about to go to work when they were confronted by the labour officer—who ordered them to leave the camp.

Roscoe was a camper who didn't work at the camp under any circumstances. He had argued with a farmer in 1972; and as a matter of principle chose not to work for a Friday Bridge employer again. Roscoe, being aged in his late sixties, had been going to the camp since the latter part of the 1950s.

Being bespectacled—and with a large beard whilst speaking like an Oxford theologian—Roscoe stated that Britain should be ruled by a left-wing dictator, adding, "Of course he would have to know what he was talking about." He added that only a fool worked hard; and bragged that it was unlikely that anyone could have done as little work in their adult lives as he. Roscoe was proud that during the Second World War his commanding officer had told him that he was the worst soldier in the British Army.

Even though Roscoe had done so little work in his life, he was, through inheritance, one of the wealthiest campers. He spent each winter relaxing in Asia until it was time to take a summer's rest at Friday Bridge Camp.

While I relished being selectively disliked, Roscoe went out of his way to annoy campers. After discovering a person's perspectives in life, Roscoe deliberately took a diametrically opposite point of view.

Regarding his early life at the camp, Roscoe said to me, "On my way to a new job I used to half hope that I would be sacked. When I arrived I deliberately started an argument with the farmer."

Yet he accusingly asked me, on seeing my presence on the camp during a midday, "Why aren't you working?"

I replied, "I've just finished the breakfast shift!"

On seeing me doing security work he asked, "What time do you finish?"

"2.00," I answered.

He looked to his watch as he stood in a hut's doorway, then said in a mocking voice, "You have to work in the cold... for another two hours... while I will be in my warm room."

There was always a tenseness during closing time at the clubhouse, the security members not knowing what unpleasant situation that drunkenness was able to catalyse... whether it be wrecked huts or assaults on people, it was our job to confront it.

But—the head barman was more interested in the sex lives of campers than security work. On patrolling the football pitch, he said, "Quick Jim... shine the torch to the field... see if there's any arses going up and down!"

We found Japanese John who was married bouncing a camper against a hut. On seeing him with this woman, the head barman instructed us to retreat. There was, it seemed, a mutual abhorrence between these highly positioned staff rivals.

Japanese John had wrongly told some Japanese campers that he was the assistant manager—and for them to report to Ukrainian Steve for work in the kitchen.

The head barman yelled at them on overhearing these campers tell Steve that John had sent them to work in the kitchen, "Go back and tell him all he is is a shithouse cleaner!"

One of the kitchen workers had been carrying a pile of plates to a door—then said in a strained voice to Japanese John who stood with empty hands nearby, "Open the door... for me... will you?"

He retorted, "The catering isn't my department." He left the wobbling plate carrier to find his own way through.

During a meal, when all the staff members met at the cookhouse, with the exception of the labour officer and his wife, Japanese John said to Blodwyn who had made the tea, "I know that everyone in Wales is called Dai... your tea is dai-abolical!"

Blodwyn replied in a deflated scowl, "Haven't you got any shithouses to clean?"

Japanese John irritated some of the campers as well as staff: once the workers had left the camp during one morning, he went into the gangers' hut and placed a boulder into an unused locker—before locking it—then placed a label with the name of a most unpopular former camper on its front.

On returning from the courgette fields, the proverbial monetary socialist went into an incandescent tantrum on seeing the identity of his new roommate.

He subsequently approached Japanese John, then asked the meaning of putting this person in his hut. John laughed.

The people that shared a hut with me didn't change much through the season. I had the company of veterans—such as John the Yank, John the Book and Fat Mac.

John the Yank, as he smoked a Senior Service between brown-stained black fingertips, trumped profusely—while verbally dreaming about suitable women he wished to continue the rest of his life with—while his body relaxed in bed.

I wasn't in my hut when Fat Mac arrived but became aware of his presence two beds away from me, during the hours of sleep because I recognized the snoring that emanated from him—which I had not previously heard since the last time I shared a hut with this camper in 1981. Then, some other people were so disturbed by his snoring that they changed huts.

Fat Mac indignantly responded on seeing them leave, "Do I snore?"

Four years later a camper on a week's holiday yelled through the snores, "I can't take anymore… I'm going to sleep outside!"

I found that I was only able to sleep during his night-time noises due to drunkenness.

John the Cowboy said of Fat Mac, who was near retirement age, "It's a pity that he doesn't snore when awake… and quiet when asleep!"

John the Book, aged in his sixties, was the camp's table tennis champion. When picking strawberries he didn't crouch like everyone else, but picked in a 'bend down touch your toes' position... all day.

He had been going to Friday Camp since the sixties—and had been known as John the Book because he read so often: titles included *The Art of Accountancy to Calculus*. When apple picking one of his hands was used to hold a book; but he did this only on an hourly rate.

John seldom spoke. Some of the veteran campers said that he hadn't talked during his first five seasons at the camp.

John exhibited to me that he followed an unusual sleep pattern. No matter how cold and wet the outside atmosphere was, John used the swimming pool at midnight. Within half an hour he returned to his bed; at 3.00 a.m. he returned for a second swim, then returned to bed; at 5.00 a.m. a third swim was taken by him.

Roscoe said of John the Book, "I remember him at Brid... over thirty years ago; his behaviour was the same.

Brid was a camp where campers in the fifties and sixties used to go once Friday Bridge had closed for a season.

Another camper who worked at Brid was PJ. I perceived him to be a refined, wealthy, intelligent person. PJ had previously travelled the world as a merchant seaman, but due to his vision becoming impaired he sought an alternative form of work.

In his early days as a seasonal worker PJ spent the whole season at Friday Bridge Camp; but during the 1980s he spent six weeks there—working as an apple picker, using these earnings to pay for his rates. During the rest of each year he lived off dividends from his shares.

Another wealthy camper was Dick the Walker, who had been spending more time at Friday Bridge Camp since recently retiring from the fire service—and he spent his winters in Asia. Dick was a phenomenal walker. He had, at the age of forty-nine, raised sixteen thousand pounds for a charity—after walking one-hundred and thirty miles in two days.

PJ and some of the other veterans said that the camp was much better in its early days—where the food and wages were far superior then in comparison to later years' standards of living.

One old-timer lamented how he was able to earn the cost of a week's accommodation after just a few hours' work in the fifties. Yet I was unaware of such a precedent during my time at the camp.

A veteran camper remembered when the labour officer and his wife had met as campers. In those days, he said, an urn of drinking chocolate was made available at supper times for the campers.

Roscoe said to me, "I have had a good life. I hear of people of my age saying that they wouldn't relive their lives… but I wouldn't mind reliving mine!"

I asked Roscoe if his life had gone by quickly.

He replied, "The past ten years have flown by…, but the years before then went by slowly. Apart from the six years in the British Army I have enjoyed my life."

The time came for me to leave the camp—in order to pursue my next seasonal job.

CHAPTER FIFTEEN

DURING EARLY SEPTEMBER I went to Kent—so as to work on the hop harvest for Guinness.

My brother David had got me this job at Tickham binder—in the region of a village named Teynham—having worked for Guinness in 1984.

At the nearby Norton plant worked another person I had known before, namely Joe whom I had done seasonal work with, both in Greece and at Friday Bridge Camp.

Since leaving his staff job at the camp in 1982 he had worked following a France-Italy-Greece circuit. Joe had done grape picking in France… apple picking in Italy… and orange picking in Nafplion. He had done construction work in Greece also.

Joe suggested that I joined him and his girlfriend—on a French grape harvest after the hops had finished.

I declined—and explained that I would be endeavouring to visit Australia.

He scornfully retorted, "You said you were going to Iceland… and you never went!"

I believe that Joe wanted me to eventually return to Greece. I had no intentions of working there again. He said, if I didn't return I would be forgotten there. I felt absolutely no desire to do a fourth season in Greece, and could think of not one good reason to return.

I subsequently philosophised: who would remember anyone once the sun had eventuated... to the state of a black dwarf?

While socializing with Joe in the nearby pub called The Plough and eating in Crispin's Restaurant in Teynham, which was situated in between the towns of Faversham and Sittinghourne, I concluded his personal characteristics were markedly different, in Nafplion, Friday Bridge Camp and in Kent.

Personally I believe that Joe didn't like outdoor agricultural seasonal work. He was attracted, rather, to the social life that sometimes accompanies this form of employment.

Whilst eating with Joe at Crispin's he seemed impressed with how well I was doing working for Guinness, with respect to when we first met during the strawberry crop in 1980.

He said to me, "I remember you when you were a villain and a nobody... and now you're eating artic roll."

He referred to me as being a villain because Tom and I had been questioned about the robbery at The Chequers in Friday Bridge village five years earlier! Even though we were innocent, Joe wouldn't believe me in this instance.

Joe said many sayings, but the one I particularly agreed with is—"The easiest jobs are the best paid... and the hardest jobs are the worst paid."

The baling of hops being a prime precedent: I had done much harder work—for a lot less pay—in other seasons.

The hop bailing was controlled by my immediate superior at Tinkham binder named Paddy. Paddy in my opinion was very good at his job as a hop dryer. He enjoyed sharing in jokes—and being part of a team consisting of casual workers, which worked well under his efficient command.

Another person who enjoyed having a laugh with us was Mick the lorry driver—who came to collect loads of baled hops. He told us over a cup of hot liquid in the tea room how the police arrived at the home of a man who had stolen a safe. Mick said, "Four coppers couldn't carry it out... so he said to them, 'Out of the way!' He then picked it up and carried it out for them."

I was impressed by the politeness of the Manager and foreman towards us. There were no threats of dismissal before we had even started to work like I had experienced in East Anglia.

At the end of the season the manager shook our hands and thanked us for the work we had done.

I left Kent during early October.

I conceded that Guinness was a good company to work for—not just because of the pay and working conditions, but because we were provided with a caravan at no cost to us.

CHAPTER SIXTEEN

O N THE EVENING of the day that I finished working for Guinness I returned to Friday Bridge Camp.

At the office the labour officer asked me suspiciously, "Been on the apples?"

"The hops," I returned.

I spent a part of this evening telling people about the indoor seasonal work I had done for Guinness.

On going to the club during my first night back, the head barman said to me at the bar's other side, "You're so lucky... if you fell in mud you'd come out with two gold watches!"

His statement represented the events of an evening—soon after I had gone to Kent, when he and Jim caught a gang of Glaswegians wrecking a hut. Consequently a fight took place in which he and Jim were charged with grievous bodily harm due to their intervention. One of the Scotsmen received seventeen stitches in a facial scar after being hit by a torch handle; and another lost front teeth.

I felt most fortunate not to have been involved with this... The pending court case would have spoilt my Australian plans.

Jim would have been better off not working on the security. He ended up being financially disadvantaged due to him having to take days off work to seek legal help. The labour officer refused to give him any financial assistance... even though this criminal charge resulted due to him doing his job protecting camp equipment.

During the following morning the labour officer asked to see me. At his office he said to me, "John hasn't turned up... Will you do the Sunday shift in the kitchen?"

The first camper I observed on pulling up the counter shutter, in the meal queue, was a man who appeared to be in a rage!

The Top Ganger seethed in a persecuted voice, "You earned seven hundred and fifty pounds in a month?"

"Yes," I replied.

"Joe... was with you?" his angry voice asked.

"Yes," I returned.

His face pleaded me to say yes, as he said, "It was really hard work?"

As his food was put in front of him I replied, "It was the easiest job I've ever done."

He made an anguished grimace before leaving my view.

He later ranted with respect to me, "How does he have all the luck?" And went on that I didn't help him in reference to well-paid work.

The Top Ganger was proud to be British—and believed that Great Britain was called as such because it was the best country in the world, apart from being such a wonderful place to live.

The Top Ganger complained to the labour officer that the courgette regular workers should be given the chance to earn good money at Ayres, Bates and Shippey's apple picking.

The courgette boss heard about this particular problem. He made a statement: "All those who have worked regularly on the courgettes since the start of the season must stay on them... until they finish."

The courgette boss had told Bates to stop employing campers—because the high earnings they made created a sense of resentment in his workers.

I also worked on the courgettes during 1985—for farmer Nelson, who farmed in the region of Outwell. The main difference, regarding work, between him and the courgette boss, is that Nelson paid at the legal rate.

Nelson, being also a director of Friday Bridge Camp, was concerned about the running of it. He told me, "I think that there's a cover up at the camp. Do you remember the trouble at the camp? I am the director responsible for security and maintenance and I wasn't informed until four days after that security trouble had happened." He was referring to the riot at the camp in 1983. He continued, "It makes me wonder if something's going on that shouldn't be... and if some people are going to lose their jobs. Some people have been doing their jobs for too long."

Nelson said that he believed the camp to be over-staffed—and that the maintenance should be replaced by contractors whom he justified would be cheaper. He maintained that this problem existed because the labour officer wanted to employ the same staff, season after season.

Nelson believed that the courgette boss wouldn't continue for much longer as a powerful agricultural figure.

He justified this view by saying, "The difference between us and him is that he is a businessman whereas we are farmers."

Nelson was responsible for the courgette boss becoming the Chairman. He gave him the casting vote during a plot by the young directors to overthrow the old chairman: Woodrow.

The new chairman had the tendency of employing locals to do jobs that had been traditionally done by campers.

One of the last jobs I did in the 1985 season was apple and pear picking at Wisbech St Mary's—for farmer Quince who paid at sixteen pounds a day.

Quince, a chain smoker, gave me the impression that he was a fair, friendly man.

He told me that in the sixties Friday Bridge Camp was the most popular place in the Wisbech area—socially. He added that the club was so full that one had to queue for some time—due to the bar being six layers of customers deep for most of an evening.

While in the morning work queue the labour officer said to me, "Back to Greece, John?"

I returned, "I'm going to Australia."

He laughed while walking away.

A camper asked me, "When are you going to Nafplion?"

I returned, "What's the point?"

I had anticipated that I would only do three seasons in Greece; I simply didn't feel comfortable about the prospect of doing a fourth. If I had done a fourth season, it would have just been for the sake of doing it... because there was nothing better for me to do!

During this stay at the camp I noticed that people I had regularly conversed with in past seasons just didn't have much to say to me this year.

During my last mornings at the camp, The Top Ganger and some others used to leave the dining room to wave me off—with his girlfriend giving me a farewell kiss; but during this season these same people remained quiet and seated as I left.

I had done something they couldn't forgive me for—I earned more money than them.

I left Friday Bridge Camp during the middle of October.

CHAPTER SEVENTEEN

DURING THE EARLY MARCH of 1986 I arrived at Cobram, Victoria. I went to the address of an office that the Australian High Commission had given to me— whose purpose was to help people find seasonal work.

A woman in this office told me that she was unable to help me, so I should go to the nearby Commonwealth Employment Service Office.

I was told at the CES office it would be very difficult to find employment on a nearby farm… but they would try and find me a place, so I should return two hours later at 1.00 p.m. to know if work could be found for me.

I felt perturbed as I waited on an exterior bench, thinking whether it had been in Kent, Friday Bridge Camp or Nafplion, that I had been told that in this part of Australia, during this time of the year, that there was an abundance of well-paid work.

While I continued to sit under the piercing sun I watched a young long-haired man approach me. He then asked, "Do you want a job? I've got two jobs… for people… My two friends said they would come with me, but let me down."

I accepted—and went three kilometres to a camp with Peter. Soon after registering at the work's office, I was given a key for room number twelve.

While familiarizing myself about the camp, I conversed with an Englishman named Ian in his hot, grey, breeze-block room. Ian told me that he had been a contractor on potato harvests in the Cambridge area. Ian added that he wouldn't work in the Fenland because he didn't want any trouble with the gangers there. Ian was on a round the world trip—and would be going to America next.

Ian said that he was fed up of living at the Cornish workcamp, but intended picking fruit for them while being based by the Murray River. Ian justified his decision saying that he would be able to choose the food he ate while living in a tent, whereas the Cornish workcamp provided three meals a day—and somewhere to sleep for fifty-five dollars a week.

Soon after I left Ian's room I saw a circle of people where two men fought within its boundary.

I felt fortunate to share a room with a person whose mannerisms suggested to me that he was a good-natured man. His name was Johnny Watson who emanated from the Queensland town of Yepoon.

During my first day of peach picking a grotesquely featured man made casual conversation with me. I later found out that he was one of the two men that had been fighting the night before. The other fighter's friends had attacked him while he was in bed, then made a mess of his face.

I thought the work—in such exasperatingly hot weather—was already hard, without being beaten, especially during the hours of sleep.

I found the wages doing fruit picking at Cornish Fruit Farm far better than I had known on fruit farms in Britain… and the cost of living to be cheaper. In Australia some of the top fruit pickers earned more than a thousand dollars a week.

Sometimes, towards the end of a working day, there wasn't enough time for anyone to complete a fresh bin—so a few of us filled one. The money earned from it paid towards that evening's drinks in Cobram.

The locals there called us 'fruit loops'—and there were fights between them and the pickers at Cornish Fruit Farm. I noticed that the locals that started fights tended to target dark-skinned Islanders.

On our days off we filled empty rubbish bins full of lager cans, then placed blocks of ice on top during the afternoons and relaxed in the sun while on the camp.

I celebrated a birthday there and was persuaded to drink so much alcohol by my companions that I ended up sleeping under a tree to escape from its intoxicating effects. I was subsequently discovered by a young man named Red… Consequently I awoke, then returned to the drinking binge which lasted for the best part of two days.

The heaviest drinker was a thirty-six year old Fin named Ilka. Ilka said that he had been the first seasonal worker to arrive at Cornish Fruit Farm during 1986, adding, "I've seen them come and go… some left soon as they saw the rooms."

Ilka who had spent six years in the Australian Navy said that he wouldn't return to Finland—because it is too near Russia. Ilka became one of my favourite friends. He had saved no money and most of his earnings were spent on alcohol.

At 6.30 a.m. in the morning he smashed at my door, saying, "Come and have a beer... or I'll kick your door down!"

On entering his room one evening I accidentally dropped a ten dollar note—to the deck. Ilka told me I had dropped the money on purpose so as to test his honesty.

Ilka gave me the impression that he suffered from psychological difficulties. Ilka said that some people could tell from his eyes that he had tried to end his life.

Ilka also told me he had killed a man in Asia... and had got away with it.

He said to me, "If anyone troubles you Johnny, I'll smash them against the wall and slice them up like peanuts!"

During the season I damaged one of my legs at work. Consequently I was provided with free medical treatment— and was paid at the equivalent of twenty pounds a day.

I received sympathy from some workers due to me receiving in their opinion such little money.

But I realized how fortunate I was to be able to work for such a good employer—who also provided high quality meals.

While convalescing I thought back four years, to 1982, when I worked at the courgette factory topping and tailing corn cobs.

There, Bald Alan told me that while working on an apple orchard, a camper fell from a tree, breaking his leg. Later on, the farmer arrived, then asked the ganger what time the camper broke his leg. "Two o'clock" was the answer given. The boss said, "Then pay him till two o'clock!" No compensation was paid.

Once the peach season finished most workers left the camp, since there wasn't enough apple picking for them at the Cornish Fruit Farm; some of them went to Batlow to work on the apples.

While I considered my options, Ilka approached me, saying, "Johnny, I've got you a job here picking apples with me."

Due to there being an interval between the peaches and apples I decided to visit Melbourne.

On my way back I stopped at Mooroopna, in anticipation of meeting someone I had worked with before.

During the early afternoon I scrutinized the outside of a bar until I dubiously approached a drawn faced man who appeared at its exterior, then said to him, "You look old!"

Brian, whom I had last met in 1983, was surprised to see me. After shaking hands, he responded to my opening remark, saying, "I'll look better after a shower."

This was the only time I had known water being suggested as a means of removing white hair.

After a few cold lagers Brian took me to his camp.

Even though Brian lived on an apple pickers' camp he was unable to work due to a leg injury.

Brian suggested that I returned to Mooroopna after my work had finished in Cobram.

Most of the people I picked apples with in Cobram were known as gun pickers—because they were capable of harvesting comparably vasts amounts of fruit. Twenty bins of apples picked in a long working day was the Cornish record.

But the most prolific workers while I was there picked between twelve and fourteen bins a day.

Yet so much of this fruit was damaged: the gun pickers threw their apples… then turned away as the fruit, leaves and wood dropped into the bins.

On the other hand the conscientious people who fussed about the bins picked considerably less.

Jack the foreman didn't like the gun pickers, shouting at some of them due to them earning high wages for bad work. One of them contemplated resigning, saying that he was being victimized.

I found it comical to watch the wife of one man, who came to help him complete his final bin each day: she chucked bucketfuls of fruit into the large wooden container. I thought back—and wondered what Monty at Shippey's and the fussy farmer I had picked apples in Kent for would have done.

During April there were only six of us living on the camp. One of them was a former bank clerk named Mick who had been picking fruit at Cobram over a period of eight years. He said—out of the many people that worked for Cornish during each season—there were only one or two faces that he'd seen before living on the camp.

Another remaining worker was named Gerri—who did fruit picking as a means of financially supporting his interest in opal prospecting. Gerri had a claim in Coober Pedy—in which he was in shares with a wealthy businessman who financed its operation, while all the prospecting was done by himself.

Gerri admitted that he hadn't made a fortune—but knew those that had. He said that some prospectors had made a find, amounting to a fortune, during their first season; while others had spent decades of searching and had imported all their financial resources into finding nothing of significant value.

Gerri talked about the various kinds of prospecting which didn't involve the machinery that he used. Some of these prospectors sifted through the left-overs that had been dug up by machine, and earned up to one hundred dollars a day.

Gerri added that claim jumping was common after people had finished work; others arrived and dug until the owners were in sight. He rationalized that it was impossible to know what had been taken out since it wasn't known how much opal was originally there.

At the end of the season Ilka tried to persuade me to join him working in the mines of Mount Isa. Ilka didn't believe in working at the same place more than once. His motto was: Always go forward... never go to the same place twice.

While working at Cobram I was told that the immigration officials a season earlier arrived dressed like seasonal workers and they caught one illegal worker.

On a farm in New South Wales I heard on the radio that an illegal seasonal worker had been wounded by gunshot— from an official's weapon. The official said that his gun had accidentally fired during the chase.

I returned to Mooroopna and subsequently found Brian's camp very difficult to find; I initially got lost during a taxi journey—whose driver said that he wouldn't go to Wales because it was a part of Northern Ireland!

I left the taxi and drunkenly walked about the dark countryside before finding a driver who knew the whereabouts of the camp under determination. During the following day I met the other people on this camp, one of whom I had known at Cobram named Bevan. Although Cornish paid at a better rate than the Mooroopna farmers did, Bevan preferred working at Mooroopna because he found the picking system at Cornish Fruit Farm to be too regimental.

Bevan, being middle-aged, had spent much of his working life- doing seasonal work. After the apple seasons in Victoria he cut sugar cane in Queensland. Bevan cut the sugar cane by using a machete and claimed that this is the hardest of all seasonal work—the earnings being fantastic. Bevan anticipated making several thousand dollars in a few months—but stressed that most of the work done on the sugar cane harvest is done by machines and rarely harvested by machete.

Another person at this camp was a young man who told me that once the apple crop finished he was going-to make money by being a professional better. This man explained that he would be a punter, not a gambler. He explained the difference—a gambler bets on chance, whereas a punter places money on the probability of sequences.

A person I picked apples at Mooroopna with was a middle-aged Kiwi hippy named Tyler. Tyler at one time had been employed as an attorney. He subsequently followed various seasonal circuits—such as the cherry crops—and subsidized his earnings by writing articles while also living alone in remote mountains for a few months of each year in a campervan.

Tyler held extreme left wing views and had been involved in a political argument with Brian, who claimed to be a socialist.

Brian said that he is a socialist—on the basis that all people are equal.

Tyler retorted that all people are not equal—but the most able people in society have a responsibility for those that are less capable.

Brian was the only person on this camp that didn't work—he was unable to due to a leg injury.

Brian was waiting for an operation to be performed on his strained leg where a bone had been damaged. This injury had been caused due to him standing too much while apple picking. I noticed when we had worked together in Kent that Brian was the first to start work and the last to leave the orchard. I also know that he didn't take any breaks between start and finish of a day's work. In the long run Brian would have been financially better off if he hadn't picked so much in Kent—so that his health would have been better, enabling him to have done the 1986 apple crop in Australia.

At the end of the apple season Brian and I went m Melbourne after visiting bars in Shepparton. Once in Melbourne we parted company—with me going to Adelaide to visit a friend.

After my visit in Adelaide I went to Perth where I stayed with another old friend.

Soon after arriving in Western Australia I went to the Commonwealth Employment Service office in Perth, which I found to be such a brightly white, clean city. But there was hardly any seasonal work on display—yet I was told of an outback farmer who had driven four hundred miles to a Perth Youth Hostel, searching for a tractor driver.

I headed north after holidaying with my friend, and arrived at the banana plantation town of Carnarvon.

I based myself for a few days at the Port Hotel while confidently looking for work. I felt optimistic since I had been told that there was agricultural employment available throughout the year, but I couldn't find a job.

Consequently, I ventured south to another coastal town, called Geraldton.

I was given a few days free accommodation by a religious group called The Potter's People that befriended me through some of its members.

While attending one of its services I found that so many of the couple of hundred or so members consisted of young people.

During a service its plump, American ginger-haired pastor bellowed, "Poor people are evil!"

Subsequently, members started to throw themselves to the floor.

As I stood watching the majority of the congregation babbling incomprehensively someone asked me, "Don't you feel anything?"

I responded, "I feel nothing."

There was a shortage of employment in Geraldon. The only seasonal work on display at the CES office was for a tractor driver to plant seeds on a farm ninety miles into the outback.

Consequently I decided to return to Carnarvon.

I briefly re-based myself at the Port Hotel while searching for work. At my fourteenth visit to an employer I saw a young man. On seeing him in the periphery of a banana plantation, a thought entered my mind: *he will give you a job.*

This man offered me a day's work.

During the chopping of dead leaves Ned invited me to his home for a meal.

He later changed his mind and told me I could work my own hours while finishing the banana thrashing work—for the rest of the plantation.

I feel that I was given more work because he felt sorry for me. I then based myself in a caravan that I rented.

The work which I could have done in ten days I did over a period of three weeks. I enjoyed working alone and being able to holiday during the same working days.

The worst aspect of this job, apart from the constant mosquito attacks, is that I went tropo: when chopping leaves I felt as if I was cutting down human beings... with a machete!

I was later told that tropo is caused by climatical changes... in which brain fluids become unsettled within subtropical areas.

After finishing Ned's work, a neighbour of his offered me the same kind of employment.

I refused on the basis I wanted to see as much of Australia as I was able to. I was confident of finding work further north. In retrospect I know that I made a mistake—I should have accepted his offer because I was unable to find employment in the north of Western Australia.

The lesson I learned from this experience is—always take work when it's available if there's no certainty of finding subsequent jobs.

After leaving Carnarvon I went north to the town of Karratha. There I found advertised a small amount of work for courgette harvesters.

Due to me finding problems regarding accommodation, I decided to go further north—to Broome.

During the bus journey I caught head lice—having sat next to a black-nailed hippy.

I couldn't even find any relevant work being advertised in Broome. It was a highly expensive touristic town whose beaches I was told were the finest in Australia. A night's stay in a tent was charged at eighteen dollars—which was more expensive than the Port Hotel at Carnarvon! I eventually found good accommodation at the Aboriginal Hostel—where, for ten dollars, three meals were provided as well as a bed.

I shared a room with one of the most fascinating people I have ever known.

The person in question spoke in an American accent and looked as if he was aged in his early sixties.

During conversation this man told me that he originated from the English town of Shropshire—and that, sixty years earlier, he had gone to America, then deceptively acquired American citizenship.

He explained: "I learned to speak American, think American and act American. I learnt the history of a mid-west town that had been destroyed by fire. I argued with the authorities after being questioned on the validity of my nationality that my records were destroyed in the fire. I was then questioned by a panel of experts. They questioned me about the town's history. I was so convincing that I won them over."

This man told me of the high quality Virginian marijuana he smoked all those years ago—adding that there is something wrong with the stuff used today since it sent young people mad.

In May 1986 this man, aged eighty-five, was still travelling.

After holidaying in The Northern Territory places of Darwin, Alice Springs and Ayres Rock, I arrived at Cairns in Queensland. I found that most people like myself were searching for work in the water industry—such as diving off the Barrier Reef.

Consequently, I headed south to a town famed for its agricultural seasonal work: Bowen.

I rented a caravan—then developed a format regarding employment.

Two young men who were touring Australia at this caravan park had found work tomato picking. They complained that their farmer sprayed chemicals on the areas that they worked at the same time that they picked.

I tried unsuccessfully to find any agricultural work. I was dismayed—since it was in June—when I had been led to believe that the tomato season would be well underway; but market economics prevented this crop from being harvested on a large scale.

Consequently I ventured south.

Soon after booking into the youth hostel at Mackay, I unpacked, then relaxed in the recreation room where a mutual recognition was observed by myself.

A man who said his name was Ed began speaking to me. He had been on Friday Bridge Camp in 1985. Ed told me that he was the camper with Stinky who had been ordered to leave the camp for working privately.

Ed explained: "I came back to my hut and there people were asking what they made. Someone asked someone what he earned. He said twelve pounds. He asked somebody else... he said fourteen pounds. He then asked me how much I earned. I said forty pounds. Next thing I knew I was told to leave the camp!"

Ed said that he was going to Bowen to harvest tomatoes. I told him about my lack of success in finding work there. He suggested that I try again.

Ed was aged at thirty-eight and had been travelling and working about the world for fifteen years. He spent six years of this time working as a sign-writer and artist in the Crete town of Aghios Nicolaos.

Ed referred to the foreign down and outs on Crete as the 'wine and cheese brigade'. He added, "They laugh at me and say there's a tourist... Because they are poor and dirty, they think *they* are the pioneers... the veterans, the *real* travellers. But what they are doing has already been done!"

We went to Bowen and I found the work situation to be the same as before.

Consequently, Ed suggested that we went North—to Ayr.

We were surprised to see such a good display of seasonal work at its CES office.

I conceived that the locals there weren't too enthusiastic in obtaining agricultural seasonal jobs—on the basis that they were advertised over a span of several days.

A job that wasn't displayed for more than a day and attracted a fair amount of attention was paid at more than one hundred dollars a day—and involved sitting on a chair by a roadside recording the types of vehicles that passed through the town.

An official at the CES office said, with regards to employment, "I decide whether a person is decent... or an arsehole. I keep a special selection of jobs for people I like!"

Some of these jobs involved corn detassling.

Due to Ed and me being assigned work as cucumber pickers, we rented a caravan.

Having done this work before, I found the toil to be all right—but it took its toll on Ed's back since he was more familiar with tree crops. After a trial, he was given work on the squash button melons—from which Ed received the sack.

We decided to make our fortunes in Central Queensland... at the Anakie Gemfields.

This area had a prospecting feel to it; names of towns in this region included: Sapphire, Rubyvale and Emerald.

We based ourselves at a youth hostel which was built, like most of the buildings in this area, of billy holders—the stones that accompany gems.

I heard of a German tourist who found a sapphire at a roadside on the way to a store. He had this stone cut into three parts; the largest section was sold for nine hundred dollars.

I had previously thought that sapphires were only blue— yet they occurred in colours like red and yellow.

Some of the biggest finds were discovered in an area of the Anakie Gemfields known as Reward.

The prospectors were known as fossickers; some of them worked full-time searching for sapphires, while others did it as a holiday.

Some mines were subsidized by allowing visitors to pay to fossick there.

It was relatively easy to find sapphires; but the main problem was finding unflawed stones. Fossickers tended to find that by the time they've paid to have their stones cut, the cost of doing so was more than the actual worth of the sapphires!

Fossickers complained about the Asian gem dealers who bought gems in the uncut state within the Anakie Gemfields, then subsequently took the sapphires to Asia where they were cut and sold as gems that emanated from that continent.

After Ed and I concluded we were not to become rich, a decision to leave the Anakie Gemfields was made.

Although Ed was born and raised in Southern Australia, he signed youth hostel books stating his country of origin was either Canada or the UK. Ed didn't like Australian traits... and couldn't bear those fellow countrymen and women that were met by him abroad on his alleged basis that they exaggerated the characteristics of their continent.

Ed believed that people with posh accents spoke perfectly—irrespective of whether they used incorrect grammar; and conceded that someone who spoke with a rough voice was illiterate, even if that person's construction of words was consummate.

Ed was also, in my opinion, talented in writing: one of his poems was about me ghoulishly eating the brains of human cadavers.

Ed and I toured the youth hostels from Rockhampton— south to Coffs Harbour.

At this hostel the warden was so impressed by Ed's sketches that he offered him three free nights for his portrait to be done.

Ed and I were unable to find work in the areas that we visited on our way there.

In this part of New South Wales there was banana growing—but we were unable to find work in July.

Ed had picked apples on a farm in the Wisbech area— where the best picker was a local woman who harvested, he said, up to fifteen bins in a day. I hadn't even heard of anyone previously in Europe who was able to harvest so many bins.

Ed decided to concentrate his employment prospects on the orange harvest in Mundabra, Queensland, while I decided to move in a southward direction.

I met Ed again—at the Dulwich Hill youth hostel in Sidney during August. Ed said Mundabra is the worst of all the places he had ever been to regarding seasonal work.

During this month I left Australia.

CHAPTER EIGHTEEN

DURING THE LATTER PART of the month that I left Australia, I returned to Friday Bridge Camp. After booking in I saw Ken outside the office. While placing a packet of tobacco into the hand of his that I shook, his gaunt face said, "It's terrible here this year!"

Subsequently Japanese John allocated a hut for me to share with some young Asian men.

After a meal I unintentionally met The Top Ganger outside the dining room where he affectionately shook my hand and asked if I had been to Australia.

The Top Ganger seemed to be morally depleted, as he told me about himself and his girlfriend being financially worse off than last year. During this season The Top Ganger and his girlfriend were told by the courgette boss that they would no longer receive free accommodation as in 1985.

During 1986 the courgette boss had utilized a machine to help harvest his crop and consequently justified to The Top Ganger that he didn't really need him any more.

As hopefulness filled his voice, The Top Ganger said regarding the courgette boss, "I feel sure that something really bad will happen to him in the next ten years."

After a few days on the camp I became aware that John the Cowboy had become the top courgette ganger. He was paid more money than the rest of them earned each.

The Nonentity Ganger moaned to me that John the Cowboy earned ten pounds a week more than he did. In fact, John was paid forty pounds a week more than what the other courgette gangers earned—approximately.

Personally, I felt that every other camper should be paid more than the Nonentity Ganger. Since being, firstly, sacked in 1983, he had subsequently been fired from the courgette fields several more times—sometimes more than once in a season; yet The Nonentity Ganger kept returning after previously saying that each season was his last one.

Some other gangers griped on about the seasonally increase in injustice that they suffered.

I believe, if people are willing to accept bad conditions, then life will just keep getting worse.

I could understand people tolerating bad conditions for a season, but to return for another one where one knew what to expect, even though there were better alternative places to work available to them, resulted in them receiving no sympathy from me.

On visiting the club I could see that there weren't many people there—which, since it was on a Saturday night, surprised me.

I discussed the quiet atmosphere of the club with Nelson while working on his courgette field.

He laughingly responded, "The reason why the locals don't go to the Club is… do you remember the lottery last year? No one ever won the three hundred pounds."

Since the autumn of 1985 I had been interested in the outcome of the court case against the head barman and Scots Jim.

While plum picking at Ayres, Jim told me about the charges against them involving three court cases that spanned through the winter months, two of which were discontinued through technicalities and ended in Cambridge Crown Court.

Jim admitted to me, although they were found not guilty of causing grievous bodily harm to some Glaswegian campers, their accusers were in the right. Jim explained that he and the head barman were found not guilty—because their accusers arrived late at Court; secondly, their thick Glaswegian accents hindered their attempt to justify their case; thirdly, the labour officer took the stand and said that the head barman had been a good employee for the past twenty-five years.

This was the second time that I had known of the head barman being taken to court—accused of using violence on campers: in 1982 he was found not guilty of causing grievous bodily harm on a young Englishman who wouldn't leave the club at closing time.

Although, due to the courgette machine, which caused less campers to be employed, John the Cowboy was the only ganger who worked up to seven days a week.

I was surprised by his success. The courgette boss not only treated him better than other gangers, but insisted that he received preferential treatment as a camper, such as John being paid a full day's wage once a fortnight when he left the camp; but the other gangers that went away for twenty odd hours every two weeks received nothing financially from him.

The courgette boss told John that he wanted to know if staff members weren't treating him well enough.

One night, John the Cowboy went to the dinner hatch and demanded more chips.

Blodwyn replied, "You'll have the same as the rest of the campers!"

John countered with, "If you value your job, you'll give me more chips!"

I discovered that his threat both upset and worried Blodwyn.

Later, John the Cowboy laughed as he said to me, with respect to Blodwyn, "The next time I went for my tea he couldn't put enough on my plate... He was shaking like a leaf!"

Both the Top Ganger and John the Cowboy operated a loan system since people on the courgettes received a ticket each day to be cashed at the week's end; some people needed money at the early part of a week. The Top Ganger, a season earlier, in 1985, charged a pound extra for each ticket he bought whereas John the Cowboy had charged four pounds; but this would have altered to four pounds fifty. If a Yorkshireman I saw selling him a ticket refused the deal firstly, then changed his mind—the dealer would justify to me.

The Top Ganger had accused John the Cowboy of being paid more than him by the courgette boss. But The Top Ganger was unable to intimidate an old land pirate like John the Cowboy who didn't care about the threat of certain people not talking to him.

John the Cowboy responded to accusations by saying, "I'm a wise fool... A truthful liar... I'm an honest crook!"

John the Cowboy always remained loyal to his employer—as long as he had been treated well, irrespective of how badly fellow workers were treated.

I had known him to hold a grudge—solely on the basis that a newly arrived camper physically resembled one of his enemies.

John the Cowboy mocked the low earnings of this camper, taunting, "There's the four-forty man... The happiest I'll be is when, suitcase in hand, he's on the four-forty train out of here!" This camper had earned four pounds forty pence for a day's work.

John the Cowboy wanted to be, in my opinion, underestimated, by his opponents—he therefore pretended to be foolishly naive. The Top Ganger had considered him to be a harmless source of humour until John had replaced him as the premier ganger. He then aggressively began to shout orders at the other gangers.

Before he had been promoted, John used to make himself useful, while the other courgette workers relaxed. At break times he used to take a brush and sweep out vans, but this was only done when the courgette boss was present.

One night at the club, The Top Ganger approached him then said, "You're aggressive in the fields!"

John the Cowboy ranted, "I'm aggressive here!"

During this time unpleasant graffiti regarding John the Cowboy could be easily read on walls.

Consequently, the courgette boss said if he discovered the perpetrators of these writings, they would be told to leave the camp.

An event happened which I perceived would make me permanently leave Friday Bridge Camp. After working for employers that I enjoyed harvesting crops for, I was allocated employment with the courgette boss.

While I stood at my designated place of work with a young Frenchwoman, I watched Japanese John look at me as he started speaking to the labour officer.

The labour officer shouted at me: "John, it's courgettes!'

I walked away—and subsequently told Ken.

Ken responded, "He knows you don't work on the courgettes!"

As I prepared to leave the camp, I could only think of one reason why my immunity had been lifted: nine months earlier the labour officer had offered me a full-time staff position which I declined to accept.

John the Cowboy

CHAPTER NINETEEN

DURING EARLY SEPTEMBER I returned to work for Guinness at Teynham in Kent. I worked again under the supervision of Paddy—with my brother David and a couple of others, one of whom had worked in Nafplion. Even though I hadn't previously known this man, I was told that he had heard of me.

I liked working with Paddy: he was down-to-earth, enjoyed a laugh and knew his job so well that it was a privilege to be able to work under such a good-natured professional.

Before starting to bale hops in the mornings, we drank tea in the canteen. Sometimes the contractor for the outdoor workers joined us with members of his family.

One morning a brother of the contractor said in an honest way regarding the outdoor workers, "I don't know why they do it... claim dole and work for us... we pay them enough."

Later that day, at both the Tickham and Norton sites, there were raids by the Social Security investigators. Consequently there were outdoor workers running about— trying to hide.

On finding policemen and social security investigators hiding in his hop gardens, our manager gave them a severe telling off—on the basis that they hadn't asked for his permission.

During our midday break the contractor's brother who had been talking to us earlier on that same day, returned to our canteen—then asked if he could use the telephone. He then telephoned the social security office—to tell them that he no longer wanted to claim for unemployment benefit.

Subsequent prosecutions did ensue; the contractor at the Norton site was given community service.

But, for the balers, 1986 was a good season, financially— for in the region of twenty-four days' work we baled in a month's work, and remunerations of about seven-hundred and fifty pounds were earned by us.

During this season Brian visited me. The operation that was done on one of his legs in Australia had been successful. Brian had returned to work on the apple farm near Maidstone—where I had harvested fruit during 1983. Brian told me that conditions of employment had improved since I was there, and that he earned up to sixty pounds a day during the 1986 season.

During early October I left Kent.

CHAPTER TWENTY

DURING THE JUNE OF 1987 I arrived at Camp Merrimac, Concord—being in the state of New Hampshire.

I had not initially intended my employment on Camp Merrimac to be a seasonal job, as such. I went there to do a job that entailed a totally different kind of work which I sometimes do. On unpacking in a wooden cabin I read black felt-written words at the back of my room's door. It was written by a past employee regarding the director that had offered me a job—which stated: "Beware of this man—he is an absolute arsehole!" The writing went on to warn one to watch his scheming ways.

As I lay at night on a top bunk bed, water, lightly but irritatingly, fell from the ceiling on to my face while trying to sleep.

On negotiating this employment I was led to believe that the living conditions were excellent—and not the Spartan ones that I found. My present conditions reminded me of those films about South American chain gangs... This camp being situated in a remote forest.

During the following day I met other staff members. I was both surprised and disappointed to find that there were so many Europeans; I wanted to live and be employed in a predominantly American workforce!

I discovered that the majority of European staff members were employed through organizations.

One person who had been employed through an organization was a young man from Surrey. He told me about camp Merrimac's orientation in London: "We were told that if we arrive at the camp before the official opening we could spend our time canoeing and using recreational facilities until the children come... and we would dread the opening of the camp. Soon after I arrived I was given a rake and told to work in the maintenance team... It was a relief when the campers arrived. All I did was pick up stones for two weeks.'

Since I arrived before the children, I lived and worked with the maintenance workers.

After a few days I was told to move into the ice hockey section—in which I would sleep in the same hut as children and work as a counsellor.

While negotiating this job I was led to believe that I would work with children during the day as an instructor and would have my own place to sleep during the nights.

If I had initially been told I would be sleeping in the same bunk house as children, I wouldn't have gone to Camp Merrimac—on the basis that I didn't know how to look after children.

Before moving from the maintenance quarters I was told by a counsellor—of The Ice Skating Camp—that the ice hockey children would be troublesome.

All the counsellors at The Ice Hockey Camp were Europeans; the group leader who was in charge of us was a

German named Oliver. Oliver's wife was American—and consequently he had settled in the U.S.A.

Oliver worked as a sports teacher for most of each year and specialized in instructing football at Camp Merrimac.

Oliver and his wife became friends of mine. I respected the order and discipline that he was able to instil in the sometimes unruly Ice Hockey Camp.

The working system, directed by Oliver, worked in an organized fashion... until a counsellor from North Carolina joined our team. This man appeared to me to be someone who made a career out of being a counsellor. While the staff tried to organize various sports games, he was most uncooperative.

He responded by saying "That sucks!" in front of the children—after a Dutch colleague made a sporting suggestion.

He was fired on the day that a Belgian counsellor arrived to replace him. I took him a cup of tea as he profusely cried at a dining room table. He whimpered, "Why have they fired me?"

I was unable to answer him. I knew that he had not only annoyed people in The Hockey Camp, but members in the maintenance team as well. Since he looked after children in the next bunk to mine Oliver asked me to keep a check on him—but I wasn't told why. I had heard him say while children positioned themselves in a circle about his bed, "I'm the best counsellor in the world. Don't bother with the other children."

He subsequently left Camp Merrimac to work as a counsellor on a camp in Maine.

Oliver explained to me why the counsellor from North Carolina was dismissed: The head counsellor had contacted his previous camp where they told him that he had been fired from there—due to him being involved in a biologically unnatural process of the sexual sort with children in his care.

Other staff members were fired—for drinking alcohol in the woods instead of being at the ice rink; few were told to go through bad behaviour on the camp.

The group leader of the waterfront was fired for assaulting a camper. He regularly humiliated his water sports staff through reprimanding them in front of campers and staff members from other departments. This group leader gave the head counsellor a telling off—due to him giving orders at the waterfront.

I was in the minority in that I considered the head counsellor to be bad at doing his work. Most of the counsellors liked him—and regarded him to be good at the job he did. At the start of the season I was also partial to him, but as my working experience with him progressed, so did my dislike for this man. He allocated so much preferential treatment—towards the Camp Merrimac staff and children—while condemning and disciplining The Hockey Camp children. He boasted that the whole of the camp was his domain—yet he didn't even visit The Hockey Camp, or go to spectate its matches.

Oliver had to act as our head counsellor. We were members of a camp, being within a camp.

The hierarchy counsellors had taken so little interest in The Hockey Camp that the assistant head counsellor didn't even know exactly where it was situated.

I liked the assistant head counsellor. He wanted to take a much more active part in the activities of the camp—but the head counsellor allowed him very little responsibility, so he resigned. Virtually every time I saw the assistant head counsellor he was relaxing about the camp—when his skills could have been used helping us at The Hockey Camp—instead of leaving the camp prematurely through frustration.

One Merrimac group leader had been assigned initially to work at The Hockey Camp; but had requested a transfer before the children arrived.

This group leader had been a camper at Merrimac and said that because life was hard for him, then he was going to make sure that children in his care suffered!

He behaved like the head counsellor and assigned himself to duties that hadn't been given to him—such as patrolling about the female section in the early hours, even though this was the work done by women group leaders.

One of his counsellors told me he could get him into trouble due to him interfering in affairs that he wasn't designated to be involved in, because the duties that this group leader was meant to perform were being neglected. This counsellor complained, "When he should be up for parade inspection, he's in bed."

A couple of ice hockey counsellors emptied two massive bags of water on this group leader as he slept. All his property, he found, was removed from his bunk, then set adrift in a boat on the camp's lake. He later left the camp without saying farewell.

A group leader who displayed more hatred to the hockey children than other staff members, was, in my opinion, as daft as a ship's cat. He had been in charge of two bunks; each group of children fought over his pornographic material that was easily seen on entering the group leader's place. When it was time for his children to leave—he hysterically sobbed.

The Hockey camp staff held a meeting with the two owners of Camp Merrimac to discuss an increase in pay. The head counsellor also attended, which surprised me, due to him taking so little involvement in the Hockey camp.

At this meeting, Oliver angrily shouted demands at the directors and asked for answers to the accusations that we were being mistreated—in comparison with our sections. One of the directors fumbled out inadequate answers, whilst the other one was calm and lucid. He gave immediate and satisfying answers to every complaint and explanation that was addressed by us—giving me the impression that he had already been asked these questions so many times during the past thirty years.

The head counsellor kept countering, "But it's their jobs"—when we asked why the hockey staff had up to a double the number of children to look after than the Merrimac Counsellors did—and, that the other camp's children came to stay for two months while we had children coming and leaving weekly—whose luggage had to be transported by us. I wanted to hear what the captain had to say, and not that which parrot wanted to talk about.

While the head counsellor flustered and was sometimes indecisive at work, the director who mattered was a professional. His command over all situations on the camp impressed me. I had not known him to panic and he gave the camp a feeling that it was secure under his control.

At this meeting, the head counsellor told us that he gave the head of the waterfront orders and not the other way about. I don't know why he told us this—it had no relevance to the Hockey camp.

I conceded that Camp Merrimac either needed two head counsellors or someone who was capable of doing the work of more than one, since our lack of involvement with other divisions created a feeling of alienation for the staff and children.

At the end of the season during late August, I stood in my empty bunk and for the first time in this season, the head counsellor entered. I thought in contempt: 'You couldn't visit while the children were here—so why are you here now?'

Overall, I enjoyed being an instructor and counsellor at Camp Merrimac. I had a good social life—having keg parties in the woods and visiting bars in Concord with other staff members. There was also much to do on the camp— such as water sports and archery, as well as the shows that were created by the director of entertainments, and nights out at the movies.

Oliver and his wife invited the hockey counsellors to stay with them at their apartment in Boston. She was to start a job in the biology department at Harvard University.

Just before we left Camp Merrimac, a French ice hockey counsellor stood on the bonnet of one of the director's big white automobiles—then urinated on it.

CHAPTER TWENTY-ONE

IN SEPTEMBER I went back to Kent to do another season baling hops with Paddy.

The only baler that I had known before was Armin; he had worked on the hops in the '86 season.

The hops caused him to suffer a horrible looking rash which also affected his respiratory system. Armin was bandaged up lightly like an Egyptian mummy when at work. He said to me that, for health reasons, the 1987 season would be his last.

Four scousers arrived at our plant looking for employment; they found jobs working in the gardens bringing in the hop bines.

Paddy told me that he was surprised, due to them telling him that they were being paid one hundred and twenty pounds a week. Paddy rationalized regarding the contractor of outdoor workers: "He doesn't pay that to his regular/workers... Some are paid fifty pounds, others get eighty pounds... While he pays his family more, some workers he doesn't pay at all! When we had a barrel of Guinness in the canteen... he caught one of the workers drinking Guinness. He sacked him... There was as argument... He then said to him he could work for him, but he won't be paid for this week... The worker was happy with that and thanked him!"

Officially, outside workers were not allowed access to the binder—yet one night the four scousers were found bedding down, near to the upstairs press. They were told to go back outside.

On going for a mug of tea during the following morning we found that the canteen had been vandalized—by graffiti. Although the contractor for the outdoor workers had no involvement at all with the baling of hops, his work was a purely external matter, he said, on seeing the drawings and writing being done by pen. He added, "They're not getting paid... I'm claiming for damages!"

Paddy told me that he not only knew of this contractor to shout and not pay his workers—but also to kick them.

Yet, for me, this season was another good one—I earned in the region of two hundred and twenty six pounds a week.

CHAPTER TWENTY-TWO

DURING EARLY JULY 1988 I went to Canada. On the second day of my arrival in British Columbia I visited someone that I hadn't met in five years.

Cecile was so surprised to see me in Victoria on Vancouver Island. Cecile told me that she thought that after our meeting on Kibbutz Haogen, she would never see me again—and couldn't give me an answer why.

While taking a holiday at Cecile's and her husband's home I did my first work—helping to construct a Mennonite Church.

I found Victoria to be the most pleasant city that I had stayed at, yet it was tarnished by the organized begging which I regularly encountered.

I learnt that Victoria had down and outs travelling to it from other parts of Canada due to its mild winters.

Cecile, who worked as an occupational therapist, told me Victoria only had three seasons—spring, summer and the fall.

Due to the clement climate at Victoria, the two main groups of visitors to this Island were the newlyweds and the nearly deads—meaning people on honeymoon and those in retirement.

At the Agricultural Employment Agency I received information on seasonal work in British Columbia, including a list of regions and the types of crops and times of harvests.

After saying farewell to Cecile I moved inland... about two hundred miles east of Vancouver to the first listed place on the leaflet.

I left the bus at Keremeos soon after daylight had presented itself again. Almost immediately my plan of doing seasonal work at all those stated places was disbanded due to the landscape having an impact on my train of thought— making me soliloquize, *I want to stay here!*

Due to the AEA not yet being open, I surveyed this new area—and deduced that the cherry harvest was the main crop being worked on.

As I walked, I was in awe of the spectacular mountainous surroundings—whose sheer appearance was natural in its exaggeration.

Once the time was appropriate I went to the AEA office. After proving to the elderly man within that I was entitled to do employment in Canada and that I wanted to do agricultural casual work, he utilized the telephone.

I heard him ask, "Paul, do you want any more cherry pickers?" Once the telephone had been disengaged he said, "You have a job a mile out of town at The Fruit Shuttle... They have some accommodation."

I then walked back along the road that I had already been crop surveying on.

I walked, thinking, this will have to be a bad job; the probability of it being a good one was like throwing a dice five times and seeing a six on each turn. I rationalized this on the basis that I had good employment with Guinness—in 1985, '86 and '87; and Cornish was one of the best employers.

I entered a fruit stand with the large sign: 'The Fruit Shuttle'—that dominated its front. I was able to see the sign from a fair distance away while I was walking along the road.

I left my luggage bags beneath a tree once the farmer's wife had instructed me where I would find her husband.

Her husband acknowledged my presence by a glancing awareness of me and got me a couple of ladders and bucket.

Soon after I began to work a couple of children called out to us. They appeared through the trees, then fetched coffee to the workers.

I sat about with the coffee with several other cherry pickers. After conversation, a man named Jacque invited me and another worker, named Ronald, who originated from Quebec and who, like me, lived at our place of work, to go that evening for dinner at his home.

Before meeting Jacque, my employer whose name was Paul, told his young children named Colin and Carol to put up a tent for me, since I didn't know how to construct one.

After a meal at Jacque's place the three of us sat outdoors, drinking lager, listening to Scottish music near to the Grist Mill. I was still mesmerized by the magnificent mountains while we drank.

Jacque commented, "I've been all over Canada... and here is the best." Jacque was aged thirty-five and lived with his wife and son. He said, "It hurts... it hurts my pride picking cherries... but I love it!"

Jacque contrasted the high earnings he had made as a painter and decorator with the wages he presently earned.

Jacque once ran a photography business on Vancouver Island—which had failed because of bad debtors.

Jacque showed me piles of wedding photographs, then elaborated, "I've got six thousand dollars' worth of photographs... what I took of people who haven't paid me for them!"

I thought to myself: could anything be more difficult to sell than other couples' wedding photographs?

As the cherry season continued I became more acquainted with other seasonal workers; one of whom came to my aid after hearing the noises I made—due to me falling off a ladder. Subsequently this man invited me to supper at his home. His name was Robbie Kilborn who had won more than three thousand races—when he had previously worked as a jockey in South California.

Robbie supported this by showing me his old tax claims and newspaper clippings of his triumphs, one of which stated 'Kilborn: The New Shoe...' This was a reference to Shoemaker. Robbie said that he had been in a movie on horse racing as well. Yet Robbie had little to show for it all apart from the memories of the hundreds of thousands of dollars he had accumulated. Robbie said that most of his money had been sapped by two divorces. Yet he told me that there were no regrets in his life—even though a leg injury had caused him to stop riding. He added, "I've had a good life"—and aged thirty-eight Robbie picked cherries!

One of the cherry pickers was disabled from working after being in a fight with some Red Indians at the bar in Keremeos known as The Zoo.

While drinking coffee at work Charles who was a Red Indian spoke of the fight, stating that eight or nine of these men attacked at a time.

Robbie commented in a reassuring voice, "I'm too fast."

During the cherry harvest, I met the most outstanding seasonal worker that I have encountered. His name was Vern Harder.

Soon after I had started to pick cherries Vern watched me. Consequently he gave me tips on how to improve my ability.

Vern differed from some of the other top crop harvesters at various places. They were suspicious of new workers, then gradually became familiar with them—to discover how much these fresh people could harvest, dread being felt by the best workers with the prospect of the recent arrivals being able to pick more than them.

Vern, being in his mid-thirties, was modest and polite. In the same time he picked more than double what the second most prolific worker could harvest—whereas at some other places I had worked there was close competition between the first and second. Whilst I knew of workers who made excuses for not picking the most, such as 'they had a late start' or 'their trees weren't good'—but, with Vern, no matter what the conditions, or how many extra hours people picked, they couldn't come close to what Vern could do.

Richard, being the second best picker, earned sixty dollars a day—while Vern made in the region of one hundred and forty dollars; whereas Charles sometimes worked several hours extra than them—and accumulated ninety dollars.

Paul, the owner of The Fruit Shuttle, said, "I've never seen anyone like Vern... He picks so much... Yet it's good quality. He's just as good on the apricots."

Vern Harder

Vern also had the reputation as the top apple picker in the Similkameen Valley. An orchardist said that when Vern picked an easily bruised variety such as Golden Delicious, out of the thousands of apples picked by him not one bruise could be found.

When I watched Vern pick cherries he hardly seemed to be moving. Yet, those who appeared the more active picked much less.

One day, as Robbie and I spoke while sitting under a tree, he said, on seeing Jacque collect the spurs from under his tree then rip them up, "That's an old trick."

Spurs were the last things Paul wanted to find in the boxes of picked cherries—because they hold the seedlings for future seasons' fruit. Only Vern picked well enough to leave the spurs where they belonged.

Once the time came for the cherries to finish, I still wanted to stay—even though there was enough labour for the next crop, the apricots. The harvesters on the apricots were Richard, Ronald and Charles.

Paul was content with this arrangement—conceding that there wouldn't be any problems—but his wife, Stephanie, felt otherwise and persuaded her husband to keep me on as a reserve.

After a short while, the three of them packed in. Richard, being a brother of Jacque's, quit on the basis that he didn't like the thinking that had to be done—to enable high quality fruit to be picked—and that Paul was too fussy.

Charles resigned a few times—but finally finished after being criticised for picking unready fruit.

Ronald also became fed up with apricot picking—and briefly left The Fruit Shuttle—but kept making short comebacks. The main reason why Ronald did seasonal work was so that he could watch butterflies. Sometimes he could be seen chasing these beautiful creatures—with a net—in between harvesting stints.

Due to the instabilities of some of his workers, Paul was prompted in saying, "It's like running a rehabilitation centre. The only reason why they work here is that you will be able to write about them!"

At the latter part of the apricot season Paul asked me to work on the peaches. I was apprehensive of such a prospect due to Paul saying that it is the most difficult of all crops to pick because of the very strict criteria for harvesting them.

Even though I had worked on the peaches just over a couple of years earlier in Australia... the selective picking I did there was for the process factory, where the standards of correct harvesting were much lower than was acceptable at The Fruit Shuttle... There, customers arrived to inspect the displayed fruit... and, would often drive back and forth, inspecting the produce at the several fruit stands in Keremeos.

Paul took pride in the quality of his fruit, insisting that only the highest standards of work were acceptable.

Paul said that the most troublesome customers were those who drove in one hundred thousand dollar motor homes—on the basis that they always expect fruit to be cheap, even though they accept that prices of other items will increase—but never fruit! Paul earned less for his fruit in 1988 than he did in 1980.

Peach picking at The Fruit Shuttle was the most challenging seasonal task to confront me. Not only were colour and size important, but the shoulders and positions of the fruit on the branches had to be taken into account. What made it such an awesome task was that I worked on several varieties of peaches, all of which had different harvesting criteria... and being in various sequences of ripening. When harvesting crops in other places my work was so mentally undemanding I could talk to other workers... But, while picking peaches at The Fruit Shuttle it was impossible for me to converse while working because of the intense concentration required.

During the first couple of days, I picked virtually everything but the correct fruit. On my initial tree I touched the shoulder of every peach.

I personally feel if I hadn't had my experience of working on various crops since 1980, I would have been lost when facing the challenge of peach picking at The Fruit Shuttle.

The other peach pickers were Ronald, Marje and Gabriella.

Marje and Ronald detested each other—consequently they worked as far away from each other as they could. Marje, being middle-aged, was working on her autobiography.

Ronald's attitude to peach picking annoyed Paul. The butterfly catcher worked until he had earned enough to pay for several lagers. Consequently he wasn't seen by us until the following day... Where concern was felt by Paul that Ronald was allowing his fruit to become over-ripe.

He announced, "I want to be known as Ronald of the Okanagen."

Paul responded, "This is the Similkameen Valley."

Ronald retorted, "I must go to Osyoos... I want to be known as Ronald of the Okanagen... the butterfly collector!"

Ronald said to me that he was looking for romance—saying, "It doesn't matter if she has a big ear or a big nose... It doesn't matter... as long as she is nice."

Ronald wrongly assumed that Gabriella and myself of being romantically involved. He said, to the amusement of Paul's children, Colin and Carol, "I collect butterflies... but John... he collects girls!"

Ronald was so obsessed with butterflies... he slept in the orchard to observe the ones that appeared at night.

I still kept in touch with Richard and Jacque—who picked tomatoes at Cawston—and socialised with them.

Richard told me that he had started the search for a French seasonal worker who had vanished from Cawston. Subsequently her decapitated body was discovered with its hands missing.

Jacque told me that during a nearby barn fire a human head was found. Both of these murders, to my knowledge, remain unsolved.

I also socialized with Gabriella—who originated from Vancouver. She studied both science and literature at a university there. Gabriella, who had worked on The Fruit Shuttle in 1987, told me that there is more to poetry than I could concede. I thought that poetry was nothing more than rhyming literature. She said that there is more to poetry than my concept; but I was unable to grasp it from her explanation. Gabriella also worked serving at The Fruit Shuttle, selling the produce.

When my time came to leave, Paul asked me if I would return for the 1989 season—and, on the basis that he expected a bumper peach crop, requested me to bring two other pickers with me.

I said to him I couldn't guarantee that I was able to bring anyone who could harvest peaches to the standards he desired out of the magnificent seasonal workers I knew. I added that I knew of seasonal workers who could strip his trees of their peaches—within days—but would pick fruit mostly of which, in my opinion, he would find very difficult in selling—due to it being damaged and unripe.

I hadn't received so much kindness from any of my other employers as I had known at The Fruit Shuttle. I was treated by Paul, his wife and children, as a family member. They often invited me to eat with them as well as taking me out for meals.

As the season progressed, they moved me into their campervan.

I left Canada during early September.

CHAPTER TWENTY-THREE

DURING EARLY SEPTEMBER I returned to work for Guinness.

At Tickham binder I met one of my closest friends, whom I had not done seasonal work with since 1980; Tom and I spoke of poignant times that had gone by.

Tom complained to me that after falling out of a pear tree at Ayres, he had developed hearing problems that gradually worsened over the next eight years.

Tom said that the noise of the binder was too much for his ears—hence he disbanded from working on the hop harvest.

Consequently, my brother David was brought in to replace him. There were three members of my family working at the Tickham binder. My brother Richard was a part of Paddy's baling team. David had recently been working on Yachts in the Caribbean.

It was an easier season, for me, than the past three hoppings, due to me not suffering any migraine attacks. During the 1985, '86 and '87 seasons I had thrice the number of attacks than I usually encountered in a hop-free environment. In 1988 I began taking the herb feverfew—

and, during the hop season, I didn't experience any migraine attacks.

Some people only take feverfew when they have a migraine. I found this to be ineffective. It is most effective if taken daily with water on an empty stomach all year round.

It was good to be able to work with Paddy again, albeit, for the last season: Paddy had decided that he was to become self-employed. Paddy had looked forward, over the years, to the hop season, to work with visiting balers.

Paddy said that his attitude to work was: "If you want a good job done... you've got to treat your workers properly or they'll do a bad job. I've been here for twelve years and the hoppings have gone usually well. Now and then you get an awkward one but the other balers will knock him into shape, because it's team work and they get the sack. But I have always spoken to people as I like to be spoken to... and that's the only way because if you don't they'll resent you and they'll do a bad job."

One of the few aspects of the hopping that I disliked was helping out the Norton balers; I just didn't like that plant.

Paddy complained, "Never have I had to have any Norton balers sent here... but every year I have to send balers to Norton." Paddy also disliked Norton—because he considered that it had been unnecessarily designed to do hard work.

Paddy said that Norton had been designed by the manager, whereas Tickham had a different architect. Consequently the manager showed a bias towards Norton— and dislike for Tickham. Norton's original purpose was, for two balers to be able to bale one hundred bales a day; but during a past season it took four balers until 8.00 p.m. to bale thirty.

At Tickham, sometimes, forty-four bales had been made by midday.

Norton didn't have anyone as good at drying hops as Paddy. Reports of improperly dried hops—and other mishaps—regularly circulated to Tickham from Norton.

Improperly dried hops can cause bales to combust. Paddy had known of bales being on fire as they were transported on a lorry to the brewery.

The mishaps that happened at Tickham were due to our negligence and never Paddy's.

Paddy hadn't made a mistake during the seasons that I was there. All his predictions and methods worked out in exactly the way he said they would.

The contractor for the outside workers held a diametrical view from Paddy's regarding the treatment of workers.

The contractor said, "I'm doing them a favour. I haven't got a worker. If they were good grafters they would be picking apples."

The contractor did have a problem finding workers. Some of his regulars had left him—and were replaced by teenagers as well as people past retirement age.

The oldest worker was a retired foreman who sharpened knives during the hop season—aged eighty-eight.

The outdoor workers didn't have much time for us balers during the '85, '86 and '87 seasons. They believed us to be over-paid stuck up students.

They were right, in the respect that we were over-paid; but people are worth whatever they are voluntarily prepared to work for.

They were wrong in assuming that we were all students. On average, the majority of balers there during my time weren't in higher education.

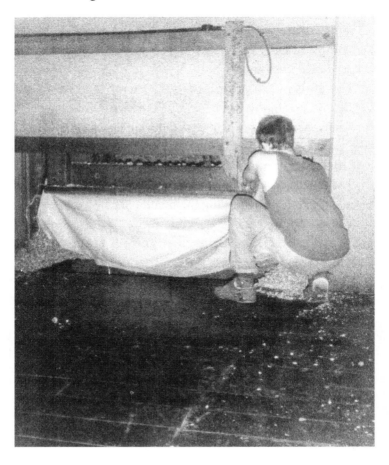

During 1988, when we didn't have much on at the binder, outdoor work was done by us, hooking on the hop bines. Only then did the outdoor workers show us respect—on the basis that we were doing work that they also did. But I didn't want their respect. I had no professional respect for them—because they chose to work for a bad employer when there was an abundance of better paid local work on orchards available to them.

The manager of the hops, was, I found, to be both honest and quixotic. He asked me if I would return each season—until 1992. During my first season I anticipated I would do four hop harvests. I would have felt uncomfortable with the prospect of doing a fifth one. Also, the manager said that the balers would earn less than during previous seasons. I would also miss Paddy—both as a friend and supervisor.

Paddy used to invite me to eat with his family. His wife would send homemade apple tarts—for the balers. When a special visitor arrived to meet me, Paddy let her stay at his house.

The foreman had got his friend, the manager, a job thirty years earlier at Guinness as a junior staff member. Subsequently, the position of manager became available; both of them went for this post. Paddy told me that the foreman still harboured bitterness—believing if he hadn't initially obtained a job for this friend, the manager's job would have been his.

CHAPTER TWENTY-FOUR

IN JANUARY 1989 I went to New Zealand. Soon after arriving in Auckland, I attempted to find some people I had previously known. I located former gang members—from my time in Greece—Rozane and Jose; he was married to her sister Kerry.

It had been five years since we last met. Kerry implied, in conversation, that the reason why I reappeared in her life was because we had known each other in a past life.

I spent several days with my friends while planning how to find my next seasonal job.

Whilst drinking in a bar with Jose at Brown's Bay, someone shouted out my name... It was a man I had known in Australia on Cornish Fruit Farm.

I made my way to Hawkes Bay by means of hitch-hiking. I rarely did this... Hitch-hiking seemed to be a novelty in New Zealand where I sometimes saw in the region of a dozen people queuing at the same area; some individuals challenged one another to a race to the next youth hostel.

A lift I received was from a red, spikey haired youth, who drunkenly called from his window, "Jump in!"

He slurred, "I've been banned from driving for four months… so I thought I'd go for a drive."

After about a mile of being in motion he ran out of petrol. While the driver staggered to nearby farmhouses with a petrol can he shouted, "I'm going to get some petrol. The people are friendly here."

I stood in the fresh, country evening air and continued to try and find a second lift. After twenty minutes of waiting my drunken acquaintance returned in a truck being driven by an elderly man.

The driver cheerfully asked me, "Do you want a bed for the night?"

"No thank you."

The hospitable man, whom I found to be a farmer, towed us for a mile to the next town. Once at a petrol station the drunken driver said, "I don't have any money." After buying him a couple of dollars' worth of petrol, we parted company.

Subsequently I received a lift from a bespectacled woman who wore a neck support. I found her conversation to be compelling. She told me, "I was a member of a convoy that was attacked by bandits in Afghanistan. In fear for our lives, all the women lay face down for five days at the back of the truck without being able to move. They robbed the men that were with us. We were one of the last convoys to go through Afghanistan before the Soviet military intervention."

Soon after I arrived at Napier, I based myself at the youth hostel there.

I found the living standards at this hostel which had once been an hotel to be better than other ones I visited.

During this time, there were a few of us looking for work while staying there.

I concentrated my search for employment on the road that went from Napier to Hastings.

There were many orchards with marvellous crops of apples—yet I couldn't find work at these places, where their owners were known as orchardists, not farmers.

After unsuccessfully trying to find work for several days I started to hitch-hike, to go to Hastings. While I waited an elderly woman walked out of an orchard to collect mail. After a brief conversation with her, she negotiated for me to pick apples.

I was the only white person to pick apples there. I worked with Indonesians, Chinese and Fijians. They joked about the whiteness of my legs; but it would only have been regarded as racist if I had found humour in their darkness—even if it had been in the friendly way that they found comedy in my paleness.

I enjoyed working with them because they were friendly and funny.

What I found to be unusual, which I hadn't known before, was that a person had been employed to train us to pick apples.

The trainer had several gangs in various orchards—and behaved as if she was someone special.

I think that people such as her are bad for seasonal work—because she was taking money that could be paid to the workers.

She worked at Ferndale orchard until we were trained to colour pick to the orchardists' standards.

In my experience many workers picked the wrong fruit by choice—and once the trainer had left Ferndale, we would pick what was right for us.

One day we were reprimanded for picking too green—but what had happened was that the Royal Galas had reverted to Imperial Galas.

I liked the trainer—but held no professional respect for her: we were told off about leaving behind ripe fruit, yet she also did this during the occasional picking that this woman did with us.

I stopped working at Ferndale, suddenly—having been told that I had to leave the youth hostel. The wardens had gone on holiday for a fortnight and their replacement said that she had no authority in allowing hostellers to stay long term.

The orchardist at Ferndale said if I returned in two weeks there would be a job apple picking for me.

I hitch-hiked south to Ashurst where I visited a couple who had worked at the same time as me on Camp Merrimac. They had returned to work there for a second season.

After a rest, I received a lift from a young man with a trailer full of furniture. He asked me if I'd help him unload tables and chairs once we arrived in Wellington. On the way he took me to his sister's home for a meal.

Once on South Island I took a sojourn at the Picton Hostel.

The next hostel for me to stay at was in Havelock. It was of particular interest, this old hostel, for me, because it had once been a school that Ernest Rutherford went to.

There I met an American hippy who had worked in the Peleponnese during the time that I was there.

On my way to Nelson a man gave me a lift, then asked as we drove south, "Have you met any druggies in New Zealand?"

Once I said no he opened a secret compartment, revealing some grass.

This young, long haired man, told me of a previous hitch-hiker he had given a ride.

"I had picked up this guy... After a while I stopped for a pop. While I was in the shop the guy drove off. Outside a bar in Picton I saw my car. I went to the police and two of them went with me to the bar. The guy who had stolen my car was at the bar. I walked up to him and punched him across the head. Another guy in the bar said to the cops, 'Did you see that? That's assault.' 'I didn't see any assault,' spoke one of the cops as they took the thief to the station."

I found the Nelson Hostel, which was a large white building, to be a pleasant place to stay. It reminded me of Festos in Athens in the respect that the accommodation involved males and females sharing the same rooms of slumber.

There I met people that I had known on North Island— such as other seasonal workers who had been ordered to leave the Napier YHA.

On my way down from Auckland so many people talked about seasonal work in Nelson, but I couldn't find any evidence of crop growing in this region. The main area of activity, I was told, was at Motueka, being about thirty miles from Nelson.

The hostel warden at Nelson told me that it would be very difficult for non-Australasian people to find work: The immigration department was keen in finding those people that weren't entitled to work due to the unions complaining that foreigners were taking their jobs. Some orchardists lost their crops because they couldn't afford to pay the unions' demands—and weren't able to employ illegal workers at lower rates. There was an immigration inspector, working full-time, making checks at orchards. On one of his raids he ensnared fifteen people who worked illegally.

As soon as I had entered the common room of the hostel, joy appeared in the face of a woman sitting at a table on seeing me. Consequently I envisaged that an amicable discussion between me and this woman that I had previously seen at another hostel would take place.

During our conversation, Birgit, who originated from Germany, asked me to accompany her to Motueka.

During the following day we started to hitch-hike; but the rain was so intense that a lucid vision of the landscape couldn't be seen.

She waited in a bus shelter whilst I fetched two cups of tea from a café. As I crossed the road from the café a man whose face suggested to me that he was a Maori shouted from the vehicle that he drove: "Where are you going?"

"Motueka," I replied.

"I'll give you a lift," he responded.

I subsequently took Birgit to the car.

Once in the car he asked for our nationalities. After answering him, he responded, "It's a pity you are not from New Zealand... I could have offered you work. My job is to drive around looking for unemployed New Zealanders and give them information on courses."

Soon after arriving in Motueka, I found the employment situation to be worse than in Hawkes Bay. The immigration had raided sporadically in Hawkes Bay; but in Motueka more regular raids of this nature occurred. Consequently, I decided to return to Hawkes Bay.

On returning to Napier, I discovered that the orchardist's wife at Ferndale had arranged for me to stay long term at the Napier hostel. The wardens, John and Jill, said that they didn't mind this arrangement.

On the day after I arrived in Napier I went to Ferndale. The orchardist told me that he had given my job to someone else. Consequently he telephoned other growers of various crops, for me, one of whom told me I could pick apples for him in a week's time.

During my wait to start apple picking, I met a man from North Wales named Tom. He regularly moaned that everyone except him had found work. Tom was so fed up that he said, one morning, that he was going to Dangesville.

I suggested to him, "Why don't you stay a bit longer? Something will turn up."

He responded in a forlorn and despondent manner, "No... I'm off... I'm going to hitch-hike to Dangesville."

It was about twenty minutes after Tom had left that Jill asked me if I wanted a job grape-picking; a grower who telephoned her just a bit earlier asked if she could find several hostellers.

I accepted, adding, "I'll go and see if Tom is still waiting for a lift."

She replied, "Don't bother... He'll have had a lift... That's his luck."

The driver who came to collect us, whose nickname was Topsy Turvey, replied to one of the hostellers in his truck who asked if there was a place for something to eat, "Phone the immigration and ask them to bring you a pie when they make a raid."

Whilst working on rows with other grape-pickers, I met an English couple. They told me that they had worked in Motueka—but found the immigration raids there to be a dangerous prospect. They had been on an orchard when immigration officials raided—and pretended to purchase fruit from a stall on the site while the other workers were deported.

I did grape-picking until my other job started.

I worked near to Ferndale picking apples from wires— where the fruit was grown in hedge-like rows.

As the days went by I realized how much better off I was than at Ferndale—where I earned in the region of sixty dollars a day; but at my new place of work my earnings were considerably more—and I didn't have to put up with a nagging trainer that contradicted her own rules.

Although I have generally preferred to harvest citrus crops than apples—I felt more comfortable picking them from wires than harvesting this kind of fruit from the way I had known in Kent, East Anglia and Victoria.

The top pickers at my new workplace harvested similar amounts of fruit as the gun pickers I had known in

Victoria—but their abilities faded in comparison with a local man who appeared in a Hawkes Bay newspaper with the twenty-two bins of apples he had picked in a day.

While staying at Hawkes Bay I became friendly with an Australian private detective named Steve. He was concerned with insurance frauds, drug sellers and marital affairs; and being uninterested in any case whose value lay beneath twenty thousand dollars.

Steve drove about in a van whose windows were blackened—and positioned within was a film recorder.

Steve told me about his investigations. "A typical insurance fraud would involve a quarter of a million dollars which the claimant got and was unable to work again. Through greed he continues to work... and I film him. He has to return the award. I don't mind this work... the people I inform on are scum!"

Steve continued: "I rarely get trouble... A Maori I was filming tried to strangle me... Mostly I only have to locate and prove where the wanted people are."

Steve was based at the YHA in Napier while trying to identify someone he had been sent to locate.

Steve had a fetish about taking women out to dinner that he was investigating. One such woman had been a big dope dealer. His evidence put her in prison for several years.

Another woman he became friendly with was investigated on the basis that her art dealer husband suspected that she was having an affair... Steve's evidence proved him right.

Soon after locating the person he had been sent to find, Steve left Napier for his next assignment.

I left New Zealand in April.

CHAPTER TWENTY-FIVE

DURING EARLY JUNE I went back to Canada.

At the Fruit Shuttle, some of last season's cherry pickers had returned; one being Charles. He had spent a part of the past winter in prison and was presently wanted on other criminal charges.

Paul regarded Charles to be more troublesome than all the other pickers put together. He was possessed by rages—and said that he wanted to kill people.

Paul and Stephanie, being Christians, believed that tolerance was a correct way to treat him.

After a couple of weeks, Charles declared that he was fed up with cherry picking. Charles wanted to return to prison—where he could lie on a bed and watch television all day. Subsequently, he set fire to his belongings, before surrendering.

Paul had only become a Christian as an adult.

Whilst being a physics undergraduate, he used to write essays which supported a disbelief in God—but as a fruit grower Paul said that the opposite view could be written by him.

I had many religious discussions in Keremeos... So many people in this area openly expressed their Christian views to me.

Another couple of workers on the cherry crop were born again Christians who had recently married.

I had watched Wayne and Tracey blissfully touch one another—as I relaxed beneath a cherry tree drinking tea.

Wayne, who was of farming stock, had been trying to borrow a cow so that he wouldn't have to buy any milk while working and living at the Fruit Shuttle.

Wayne told me that he hoped his future entailed missionary work with native Indians.

During a break Wayne gave us a religious address.

Consequently, Richard who I had known from last season, snapped back, "I don't tell you what to believe in, so don't tell me!"

Another couple, namely, Ken and Lana, who originated from Castlegar, found cherry picking to be unprofitable. After a few days of work they left Keremeos.

Soon after they had gone a mother and daughter arrived to work on the cherry harvest. Jackie, being the mother, had packed in a job as a dog patrol officer—and due to her hearing on the local radio station in Castlegar that cherry pickers were wanted in Keremeos, she and her daughter Marilyn decided to try doing seasonal work.

They said to me that Ken and Lana who they knew from back home were working in this region.

I told them that they had worked at the Fruit Shuttle. I added that I was supposed to meet them for a drink at the Legion Club—but they didn't arrive.

Jackie told me that Ken, being a cocaine dealer, was hiding from another drug peddler that he had double crossed. He had run Ken's vehicle off the road during a shotgun attack.

The oldest worker at the Fruit Shuttle was a sixty-eight year old man known as Blackie.

Each day Blackie visited the other seasonal workers and said to them, "Are you making it pay… Hard at it?" He was concerned with the amounts that everyone picked. It's a question I never asked—and whose answer was one that I didn't relish giving easily, except to those that I respected as seasonal workers.

As the season progressed people who said that they would stay until the end left prematurely. Wayne and Tracey were going to do peach picking—but finished during the cherries. They subsequently found jobs working as cowhands.

Jackie had brought a dog to the Fruit Shuttle. During a day's work, she warned us that there was a most dangerous animal nearby. Her dog had two howls that it made: one was made when a coyote was in the proximity; and the second one had been sounded in my presence—warning that a grizzly bear was nearby.

Last season a relative of Paul's took a walk up a nearby mountain—and a grizzly bear ran past him, then subsequently opened an irrigation pipe and drank water from it.

Eventually I became the last seasonal worker living at the Fruit Shuttle—having worked on the apricots, damsons, peaches and apple harvests.

During the apricots I was introduced to a former pastor who had served at the Menonite Church that Paul and his family attended. The fruit that I picked for him was placed in a truck near to the corpse of a twenty-one year old man he had collected after the man had been killed in a swimming accident.

The Pastor had previously worked in a Jail. During this time a prisoner had stabbed him. Once medical attention had been given to the wound it was established that he had cancer. This was successfully treated. The pastor rationalized that if he hadn't been stabbed his cancer may have become too progressed to be successfully operated on. Consequently he regarded this to have been divine intervention.

Just before the peach harvest was to start, Paul arranged for me to visit his parents in Kelowna.

I particularly enjoyed meeting his father who was a Scottish medical doctor. I had known him at the Fruit Shuttle where I became intrigued whilst consuming various alcoholic drinks with him about the work he had done in Africa—amongst other things.

I left Canada in September after taking breakfast in Vancouver with Gabriella.

CHAPTER TWENTY-SIX

IN THE JUNE OF 1990 I returned to work at The Fruit Shuttle—where I harvested cherries again with the likes of Blackie and Richard. There were also new workers such as Phil—a construction worker by trade but who had sought seasonal employment due to a sparseness in his original job.

Jacque, whom I had known during my first season in Keremeos, had returned to work at The Fruit Shuttle.

While in Keremeos Jacque pretended that he wasn't a French Canadian. He justified this on the basis that it was found that a human hostility to his people in this region was exhibited.

Phil contributed that in one nearby Okanagon town French Canadians had been run out of the area.

A red-haired, bushy bearded prospector named Alan suspiciously, at times, watched the other workers, but didn't speak to us.

Paul said that Alan worked for him... until he had made enough money to return to the Yukon to continue his gold prospecting.

Phil, at one time, had worked transporting fruit to the Yukon—and said that was so uninhabited that he sometimes saw just one other vehicle during a day's driving.

Phil told me that not far from The Fruit Shuttle, several years earlier, a murdered seasonal worker was found in two plastic bags—whose distance between each other indicated that he had been butchered. His killer was subsequently brought to justice.

I was introduced to Phil's cousin who was named Craig. Craig had turned away from his wealthy family whose head was a doctor, to live a Spartan life, alone. Another cousin of Phil's, an Australian, attempted to live the way that Craig did—but discontinued after a fortnight on the basis that it was too tough for him.

In the remote mountains surrounding Keremeos some Vietnam veterans lived as well.

Craig's personal transport consisted of a canoe which he used to sail on British Columbian waterways to pursue various harvests. Although Craig didn't work at The Fruit Shuttle, he knew a couple that picked cherries there that I hadn't spoken with.

Craig had said of Rodney, the male part of this couple, that as soon as he arrived at a new harvest, workers were told by him of his wage which consisted of forty dollars—being made in an hour pruning apple trees. Craig said that in the twenty years that seasonal work had been done by him, he had never heard of anyone earning anything near this wage.

Consequently Rodney refused to speak with those who disbelieved his claim.

Subsequently, I asked Vern for his opinion... since I was told that he was also a very good pruner. Vern, who pruned fruit trees during a part of each winter, said that it was possible to earn forty dollars... but just for one hour.

During the other crops I was very much alone in the orchard—with the exception of Vern who worked on some apricot varieties.

During this season I was able to do something which I had not been capable of during the past two seasons—being able to ascertain whether the different peach varieties were ripe just by touch.

I also worked on Paul's apples. He said that there wasn't a picker in the Similkameen Valley who could pick more than six bins of apples from his trees in a day.

This wasn't because of the quality of the crop, which had been good, but because of the arrangement of the trees. Paul attributed the sequence of trees growing too closely together to the greed of the last owner of The Fruit Shuttle.

Vern didn't like Paul's apple trees because there was too much moving about—for the fruit.

I felt that mountaineering equipment such as a rope and hook could be suitable to tackle the most extreme branches.

I experienced in this season the same kindness that was known to me during the past two seasons—by Paul and his family.

During the sixties Paul and his future wife had travelled about the world—and had experienced the popular cultural routes of Asia. Consequently Paul concluded to me, "There's no other way of life as easy as travelling."

CHAPTER TWENTY-SEVEN

IN THE JULY OF 1991 I went to New York. Subsequently I visited a child that I had looked after at Camp Merrimac. He had invited me to take a vacation at his family's home in East Brunswick.

Afterwards, I returned to Vancouver where I spent a night at Gabriella's apartment; we had also met during the past two seasons.

On arriving at The Fruit Shuttle, Paul told me that the peach crops had been devastatingly damaged by a harsh cold winter—and Osyoos was the only region of the Similkameen and Okanagan valleys that hadn't been badly affected.

The cherries, though, had remained relatively unscathed.

During this year I met up with people I had known during past seasons... such as Ronald the butterfly collector; he had been fruit picking at Summerland.

Jackie paid me a visit and invited me to stay with her on the way to my next place of work.

Phil, who came to see me, told me of a local schoolteacher who had tried to prevent fire fighters from watering his burning log cabin—because, inside, were electrically grown two million dollars' worth of marijuana plants.

Richard had also got into trouble with the Royal Canadian Mounted Police—for growing illegal plants. Richard was so proud of his pot plants. He invited me to see these and had his neighbours watering them when he went away on vacation... until someone grassed on his grass. Richard, who smoked five joints a day, claimed that grass made him pick cherries better.

I went to Church in Kelowna with a local man named Brad who was of native Indian descent.

All the women there wore hats and remained silent during the service.

Brad explained this by showing me a passage in which the Bible states that women must wear hats in church; and to be silent.

I think that this holy book is the most selectively used set of religious teachings in existence.

After bidding farewell to my friends in Keremeos, I ventured east to Castlegar—where Jackie met me then took us to her remote home in the Kootneys mountain range.

Jackie didn't live with other people; her companions were dogs, rabbits and a de-scented Skunk that lived in burrows beneath her home, and made nocturnal appearances. She kept her skunk separated from the dogs because it would attack them. Jackie added that skunks also attack humans—especially if people are seen running—and a grizzly bear will avoid a skunk in its path.

Where Jackie lived there were black, brown and grizzly bears. She explained that the humps on the grizzlies' backs distinguished them from brown bears. Jackie concluded that grizzlies were very unpredictable. On cutting rhubarb in her garden Jackie had felt that she was being watched. On turning around, several yards away a grizzly looked at her—before calmly moving out of sight. Jackie, though, knew of people who had been horribly mauled by this kind of bear.

Jackie was dismayed regarding the lack of responsibility of the occasional picnickers who camped in the woods above her home—due to them leaving food about their tents.

Jackie said that people should keep their foods concealed and placed partway up a tree. She added that some people were surprised to be awoken by a bear ripping through their tent—but it was because it had smelled the food within.

Jackie added that farmers have found grizzly bears sleeping in pigsties—after eating the feed.

When we went outside, Jackie had a rifle on her shoulder. She told me of a man who lived for most of his life in one area. During a walk, he turned a corner of a pathway on his way home, and was attacked by two awaiting grizzlies. Even though this man consequently lost body organs and an eye, he considered himself to have been fortunate.

Jackie said that people were particularly in danger if they happened to surprise them.

Jackie who was of Cree Indian descent was aware that some big game hunters were attracted by the elk that lived in the Kootneys where Boon-Crockett records have been achieved.

Jackie, who had as a young woman worked as a model, drove me about Castlegar to see quixotic homesteads of the Doukhobors.

Jackie told me that the Doukhobors had originally arrived in North America from Russia. Their descendants detested their history and had set fire to a museum that exhibited it.

A branch of the Doukhobors known as The Sons of Freedom were repelled by materialism and lived in Spartan conditions. They stripped naked before setting homes on fire. Jackie explained that they did this as a means of cleansing. She added that on one occasion police had arrested some naked Sons of Freedom; once in the car they set fire to it.

Jackie told me that orthodox Doukhobors were money mad—and the most shameful thing that could happen to them was poverty. Poverty in this community resulted in people who lost their wealth being ostracized.

Jackie said that Doukhobors tended to be pastry-faced people who spoke in Russian accents—and couldn't look others directly in the eyes during conversation. Their main food consisted of a high butter diet. Many of the women were drastically overweight and dropped dead during middle-age. Some of the old Doukhobor women performed witches' rites in graveyards.

The Doukhobors didn't use guns because of an opposition against violence—hence they would rather pitchfork someone to death. The orthodox Doukhobors had operated a highly successful jam factory. This was subsequently set on fire by The Sons of Freedom who justified their act by saying it was done because of the love they felt for them.

Jackie told me that the biggest regret in her life was getting married: during the sixties she had done exceptionally well as an undergraduate in an American university—and dropped out of her studies for the sake of a marriage that had failed.

CHAPTER TWENTY-EIGHT

DURING THE EARLY PART of August I arrived at the Minnesota town of Waseca to work on the corn harvest for Kraft Foods.

After registering with the human resource manager I was designated a room a few hundred yards away in a university block. Having arrived later than most of the other workers, I was fortunate to be placed in a room alone.

On the following morning well over a hundred seasonal workers gathered in a lecture hall to be addressed by the human resource manager.

During the afternoon I worked de-husking corn on a conveyor belt where I was supervised by a man named Antonio—but our working relationship ended during my first day.

The secretary requested to see me at the end of my first shift. She said to me, "Your job has changed... you will be doing sanitation relief."

Subsequently a Tibetan man who had been de-husking with me said, "I asked three times... at the office for your job and she said that she didn't have the power to give me it... and there wasn't a job left in sanitation; yet as soon as you start working here, you are given it!"

My new job entailed supervising a table of cob-selectors at a conveyor belt—allocating, in turns, their breaks, and making sure that the corn was correctly placed into the saddles.

Conversation was unsustainable while working since we wore hearing protection—hence I spent several weeks working with the same people without hardly knowing anything about them.

My supervisors were Hazel and Kathy. Hazel was a tough no-nonsense woman, being near to retirement age. Initially we didn't get on—even though I respected Hazel professionally on the basis that she made the operation run efficiently and took full responsibility for the actions she chose to implement rather than force others to take the blame when anticipated choices were unsuccessful. As we continued to work I formed a cordial relationship with Hazel—and our friendship still continues.

Once I finished running a table of cob-selectors each day I joined other workers in the sanitation crew, chemical cleaning. This is where more accidents occurred than in any of the other divisions, partly through tiredness and because we worked with some dangerous chemicals at times.

I was almost killed while using a high power hose to spray down the double duty conveyor belt... Due to a brief lapse in concentration my apparatus was dragged from the wall connection... Then the conveyor belt pulled me as the hose was whipped into it just as I let go of the instrument. The hose had jammed in the belt, causing it and the plant to close down.

I was worried because I conceded that the season would be ruined due to my tired lack of equanimity. Fortunately the plant resumed to operation after a few hours, due to the engineers having removed the hose.

Although there were so many people working at the plant that lived in university accommodation, I found, at times, a sense of social isolation. This was partly because since the plant operated through most of the hours of each day, some of my neighbours worked on different shifts.

Antonio was one of several persons that I became friendly with during the six weeks and five days I worked for Kraft Foods. He behaved as a guardian to the young black workers living on the university block. Antonio, aged in his thirties, sometimes sent food to my room, although I ate out alone most nights.

In appreciation for the kindness that Antonio had shown me, I invited him to join me for a meal in a hotel. Antonio who previously worked as a sociologist had been walking one evening through Waseca when some white men shouted racist comments at him from a traveling automobile. Antonio later saw these four men drinking in a bar. He asked them what they wanted to drink. Once they had received their drinks, Antonio said to them, "I'm the guy you called a nigger… Enjoy your drinks."

Antonia joked regarding my promotion from dehusk to sanitation relief: "During the first day you were de-husking with me… and on the next day you were wearing a helmet, goggles and waterproofs."

I responded, "We wear goggles because they make us look cool." He laughed.

Antonio disliked receiving sycophancy from non-blacks. He complained to me about an Hawaiian worker who was trying to be cool with the blacks. Antonio added, "We don't like it."

This Hawaiian worker often complained about the conditions of work at Kraft Food… Having heard that I had worked in other areas, he responded, "Birdseye is the worst."

I responded, "No, it's one of the best." I was able to appreciate how good a company Kraft Food was… having worked in comparatively drastically bad food processing plants in East Anglia.

At the official end of the season binge on the 15th of September, workers cheered. Antonio, who was going to work beyond the official end of the '91 season, changed his mind due to his girlfriend arriving at the plant.

I continued working until the 20th. I subsequently returned to New York.

The main difference about working on the corn harvest at Waseca and at any of my other seasonal jobs, was that I earned considerably more there than I had first anticipated. Due to being promoted and receiving a bonus for lasting until the official ending—my original perception, that I would earn seventeen hundred dollars, changed to the eventual acceptance that my earnings were almost double this.

CHAPTER TWENTY-NINE

IN THE LATTER PART of October, 1992, I went back
to East Anglia with the intention of finding work on
winter crops. My plan regarding cold weather seasonal work
included a visit to the southern Lincolnshire Fens.

I found this area to be more picturesque than the Wisbech
Fens. Handsome stone cottages dominated much of the
architecture between Peterborough and Thurlby.

Soon after arriving at Thurlby I based myself at its youth
hostel. On my second morning in this cold, flat area, I went a
couple of miles to the town of Bourne.

At its job centre agricultural jobs, such as the hoeing of
crops, were displayed; but I wanted to harvest vegetables. I
remembered Glasgow Karl telling me at Friday Bridge
Camp that when he spent the winter of '84 working on the
leeks at Holbeach, earnings of between twenty-eight and
thirty-four pounds a day were made by him.

On reading several regional newspapers, I saw a good
supply of advertisements asking for winter crop workers—in
the areas of Stamford, Sleaford and Spalding.

I made contact with a gangmaster who wanted sprout
harvesters. He offered me a job—but there was a delay
before work would commence.

While waiting to start work, a married couple at this youth hostel invited me to join them on a journey to Wisbech. This was one particular place that I had no intention of going to... I had gone to Lincolnshire to start afresh. Due to a pang of nostalgia being felt by me, I drove to Wisbech with them.

John Mallon

While walking through the new shopping centre in Wisbech a lace from my footwear became loose. As I tightened the lace on my black, steel-capped boot, I looked from where I sat—then believed that I recognised someone who had aged considerably since we met last, six years earlier.

I followed the limping man until he entered a betting shop. As I closed the door, Ken, being in his mid-fifties, turned, then said as we shook hands, "You're the last bloke I'd expect to see here!"

I replied, "I'm just passing through. I thought you would be in Greece."

Ken responded, "It's all changed... I haven't been there for a few years." He later told me that much of the seasonal work in Nafplion was done by eastern Europeans.

I asked him about John the Cowboy, and was told that he was apple picking at Woodrow's.

As I entered the fruit laden woods, loud conversation and laughter became apparent.

On viewing me John didn't instantly recognize my sudden appearance as he looked down from his ladder. He then said in an unsure voice, "Well... John Mallon... I never thought I'd see you again!"

I responded, "I am surprised to see you and Ken. I only came here because I was offered a lift to Wisbech. Ken told me the camp's open."

As the Cowboy descended to my level, he added, "It's all changed. There's a. new owner. He's a good man. Where are you staying?"

"I'm based near Bourne."

"What you doing in Bourne?"

"I will be doing winter crops."

"Why don't you work here? I'll ask…for you."

I finished our conversation with, "I'm going to visit the camp."

I stood at the camp's main opening—as the dreary wind blew through the grey atmosphere. I thought about the people that had entered and left, some of whom I knew well while others whom I had only just seen, yet still remembered. I thought of the forgotten campers who believed that they'd always be remembered as legends.

On arriving at the kitchen, Ukrainian Steve grunted in a surprised way on seeing me as he prepared sandwiches with young men and women. I thought back to when others had worked there—then asked where other various people were.

He replied, "They've all gone."

As soon as I saw John the Cowboy he said, "I've got you a job… you got me work in Greece."

"Thank you," I said. "I'll bring my gear."

On returning to the camp with two dark luggage bags, John took me to meet the manager.

On paying fifty pounds for a week's rent, the manager said, "You're with John… see Ken and he'll give you your own room. Also, you don't have to eat in the dining room… eat with the staff."

John took me to my accommodation—which was luxury in comparison to other places I had slept—on the camp. I had two rooms—one to sleep in and the other I used as a study. This accommodation had once been used by a senior staff member when I was last on the camp.

John told me that this person and another staff member had recently been sacked. They were caught fiddling—which involved foreign currencies being conveyed in the club and camp shop to campers and staff—as sterling. Also, property that had been stolen from campers was on sale at the camp shop.

The Cowboy gave me an example: "My jumper went missing off my bed. The next season it was in the shop. I said, "That's my jumper!" The sales assistant said, "I found it in the bin." I said, "You didn't find that jumper in the bin. It cost seven pounds." I showed her the label with Konamara on it. I paid her two pounds… for my own jumper!"

He continued, "I remember Karl's boots went missing outside his hut. The next year they were in the shop. *He* had to buy them back."

On seeing me laugh, John gave me more examples.

"He was caught giving foreign coins behind the bar. Kevin couldn't see well and looked at his change and found German coins instead when he put out his money to count on the table. Kevin said he wouldn't drink in the club again! He went to The Sportsman." Kevin was also known as Big Kevin—a former Yorkshire coal miner.

John added, "I caught a bus outside the camp. I went to pay and gave the driver a handful of Spanish coins. I never felt so embarrassed in my life! I knew that I got the Spanish money in the club. I hadn't been anywhere else. So they set a trap."

I thought back to the courgettes—then asked John about this crop. He explained to me that soon after I left the camp in 1986, the courgette empire collapsed through financial failure. Consequently the camp was eventually sold.

I asked about various people who had worked as courgette gangers.

The cowboy answered, "They came back the year after the courgettes went bust... They didn't work... They only stayed a week... No one wanted them."

I had sometimes wondered that why in 1986 John had replaced The Top Ganger as the number one ganger. John told me that Charlie, like a gypsy, had waited, from 1983, to activate revenge—after The Top Ganger had caused him to cut courgettes while his truck was being loaded. In 1986 Charlie deliberately damaged courgette plants—then threw crates of vegetables into this region. Charlie subsequently told Gus, "Look what The Top Ganger's done!"

John and I worked at Rowley's with PJ and a local named Brian. We picked Grenadiers and Bramleys.

PJ had stopped being a camper—due to the camp having a new owner who catered almost exclusively for young campers. PJ lived in a caravan at the orchard.

PJ was like the Cowboy and Brian—in the respect that they were aged in their mid-sixties but he hadn't noticeably aged since I worked with him at this orchard in 1980.

In late November we picked potatoes—and were paid for an 8.00 a.m.—5.00 p.m. day, the same amount that was paid to us for apple picking, approximately twenty-one pounds.

I found potato picking to be far more physically strenuous than apple picking.

The tractor churned up rows of the vegetables—while John, PJ and I shared a row.

PJ—who was an expert on potato harvests—said picking these vegetables by hand had become a rare kind of employment and only happened on small plots.

What made this work so hard was, we had to stand and bend without the crouching—like in strawberries—because the potatoes were easy to take from the moist soil. The moist soil pulled us down, causing our backs to strain to a maximum arch.

We were only allowed a midday break. If we could have had a rest for a few minutes in the morning and during the afternoon so as to take a drink, I believe that the three of us would have worked better.

PJ—who had been a joint ganger in the late fifties-sixties picking outfit known as the PJ-Mick Cullen potato gang—said that women were the best potato pickers.

PJ told me of a compliment paid to him by a woman who said, "You are so good…you can work with us."

But John the Cowboy said the best ground worker that he ever encountered was Mick Cullen.

After finishing work on the apples and potato crops, I attempted again to find work on the winter harvests. I was unable to obtain a place in the gangs being run from the camp, who were to work up until Christmas due to their ganger terminating their employment in late November—suddenly.

These people earned in the region of sixty pounds a day on the sprouts—some of them working throughout the hours of darkness in the fields. I was told that some vegetables are harvested at night because frost enhances their flavours.

During December just several staff members and I remained on the camp, two of whom earned forty-two pounds a day at a processing factory in March. The manager allowed me to stay on the camp for twenty-five pounds a week. He asked me if I would return during the start of the 1993 season—to run the dining room. I believe I was only offered this job because John and Ken were friends of mine.

During the 1992 season I met other people that I had previously known, one of whom was Andy who I hadn't met since 1984—when he was ordered to leave Friday Bridge Camp. It was an unintentional meeting in a pub at Wisbech. He had arrived in the capital of the Fenland for one weekend after several years of being away.

Andy bought me an orange juice while we talked about people from our common past who had died. Andy told me that he was living in Amsterdam. He told me of other people I had known in Greece and at Friday Bridge Camp that were based in the Netherlands and had worked on the bulbs.

Andy, though, couldn't grasp what I told him about the concepts of seasonal systems that I had experienced away from Europe.

He had been a friend of mine in the early eighties—but was an acquaintance in 1992.

I also met Isobel in Norfolk who I became friends with in 1982 on Kibbutz Hukuk.

During December the rainfall was so profuse that much field work had become cancelled.

I obtained a list of gang masters from the Wisbech job centre. I contacted most of them—but only one offered me work; this was harvesting leeks near Boston.

I got picked up outside the camp. While the van drove for well over an hour, I was surprised that no one was collected in Wisbech—only in March and lesser known places were workers taken aboard.

We stopped at a field. As others got out the driver who was named Daniel told me and a few Polish men to stay in the van—we were to do sprouts. He drove us to a factory called Coolies—then quickly left.

The factory was the most Spartan that I had encountered. Huddled in the cold were men and women whose dress suggested to me that they were of a West Indian culture, sitting and peeling sprouts.

I felt very disappointed while dressed in full waterproof gear as I sat by the Polish men—peeling these green vegetables that I wanted to harvest.

Nothing was explained to us regarding payment. As we continued to work I ascertained by the general pace of peeling that it would be difficult for anyone present to earn more than several pounds in a day.

The owner of the factory spoke individually to us—trying to make us work faster. He addressed us in a manner that suggested that we didn't adequately understand spoken English. He was surprised when I spoke in English to him. I asked, "How are we being paid?" I personally believe we should have been paid at an hourly rate.

He replied before walking away, "I don't know!"

I was suspicious—why weren't any locals working there?

I asked the ganger of the West Indians how much they were paid. He refused to say.

The friendly Asian ganger told me that he and his gang left Birmingham at 1.50 a.m. and returned home at 9.00 p.m. of each day.

The toilet facilities at the factory were so bad that the West Indian ganger advised it would be unsuitable for me—so I used a field.

I felt guilty not being able to wash my hands—but there weren't any washing facilities.

On seeing the driver who had returned to collect us, I complained to him: "I was told I would be picking leeks."

He seemed surprised—on the basis that I didn't sound like an illegal immigrant. He replied in an apologetic tone, "I'll see what I can do for you in the morning."

On returning to the van, the locals I had earlier travelled with laughed at me.

While some of them made racist comments against the West Indian workers, one of them said, "Where you've worked is the worst place... but we're alright... I work for this ganger right throughout the year."

A middle-aged woman said to me, "I know what it's like... I worked there... Me and my friend were the top earners... we earned ten pounds a day; we asked for day rate... they said no. Since the Pakis have worked there the pay has gone less."

CHAPTER THIRTY

I N THE EARLY JUNE of 1993 I arrived at Friday Bridge International Camp—to run the dining room.

The manager looked at my black steel boots as the sun exaggerated their shine. He informed me that John and I would be working together in the dining room that evening.

I also found that I would be looking after the men's huts—and would be given an assistant to help John and myself.

At this time of the season the campers worked on the strawberries. On speaking to them, I discovered that wages of between seven and forty-five pounds a day were the polarities of earnings. I was surprised to find that there was only one remaining strawberry grower in Friday Bridge village—and the locals were paid at the same rate that they worked for a decade earlier.

I found my work to be often stressful—due to the paranoid behaviour of the manager regarding the regular checks by external inspectors.

Also, a Belgium television crew arrived on the camp— after campers had complained to the media after returning home.

The manager showed this crew the best room which was used by northern Europeans. But the crew later returned, without permission, and went to a dilapidated hut—where some Spanish campers complained to them about the Spartan conditions and the comparative hefty rent they paid.

Friday Bridge International Camp catered mostly for foreign campers under thirty years of age. These people had to pay for a minimum of three weeks' stay plus administrative costs.

A German woman was so upset by the conditions such as food and showers, that she decided to leave during her first week… but was refused the refund for the remainder of two and a half weeks. She tearfully said to me, "I have lost this money… I cannot believe people live in this country like this."

A Dutch friend of mine named Marian said that her three-week stay at the camp was brilliant.

Whilst some campers lived in pleasant dry huts, others lived in dismal waterlogged conditions: on sweeping out A 32 I found that water had washed through the wall, going beneath beds and then soaking campers' belongings.

On the 20th of June I sat on a bed and drank tea from a flask in A 30—thinking this is the room I first came to exactly thirteen years ago. I looked to the same spot where a puddle of water had been in 1980.

An Italian camper named Mauro complained, "There is water!"

I returned, "You should be fortunate… to have a shower—you have fresh water in your room." He smiled.

In another hut an Italian camper moaned that the windows were nailed closed.

I responded, "It's to prevent you from escaping."

A woman named Laura with other Spanish campers asked me if I knew of other camps like Friday Bridge in the world.

I replied, "Yes... there's one in Poland—its name is Auschwitz." They laughed.

Some campers were angered by the concept that employment was unfairly allocated—so they slashed the tyres of a coach and stuffed grass into its petrol tank.

Yet the office staff said that jobs were fairly distributed—and countered by saying that when people claimed employment discrimination, the same people worked every day because employers requested them.

In the seventeen weeks I was employed as a staff member I conceded that work was selectively designated—finding that there was a bias towards Eastern Europeans such as Latvians, Russians, Slovakians and Bulgarians—while the Spanish didn't receive anywhere near the same regular employment.

On visiting the huts each morning, I saw the same Spanish without work for weeks.

Two Spanish women named Elana and Paloma complained to me that their employer had been satisfied with them and had told the labour officer that he wanted these women to continue working for him—yet on examining the worklist they saw that their names were blanked out; hence they didn't work.

What I preferred about the old labour officer was that he didn't make excuses for overtly showing various campers favouritism.

The camp bad become disadvantaged in that there wasn't enough work to sustain the requirements of campers—as did the courgettes in the old system. English classes were available for a fee to the unemployed.

The Ghanaians were people who worked regularly, earning twenty pounds a day harvesting cabbages—a commitment in which they were able to work seven days a week.

Personally, I hardly knew any of the employers in 1993. Most of the people I had worked for in the old system no longer employed campers, or had discontinued doing agricultural work.

The campers in 1993, mostly, worked away from the Wisbech area; some going as far afield as Great Yarmouth. One gang from the camp that worked in a factory there earned three hundred and sixty pounds in a week.

Other high earners were in the Bulgarian celery gang— whose members earned in the region of three hundred pounds in a week.

A Siberian named Alex complained to me that the Russian gang that he worked in earned between eighty and a hundred pounds a week; whereas a season earlier while working for the same employer, wages of between two hundred and fifty and three hundred pounds a week were made by him. Alex said the reason for this is that last year he picked fields that hadn't been already harvested; but a year later his gang worked in fields that had already been cut by a British gang—followed by various Commonwealth workers.

A New Zealander who worked for the same contractor as Alex told me that while working in the Polish gang he earned less than ten pounds a day.

This man was fortunate because he earned his keep which would cost fifty-five pounds a week normally—washing crockery after work.

The chores which so many campers did for their keep varied in sheer favouritism—regarding their disparities in time length.

Ken said he knew of some who earned their accommodation by cleaning a bus once a week; and another who cleaned three toilets an evening—while others served food each night; and some others did chores that took a few hours of every day to do.

I found that during my first week, when I too was working just for my keep, I did more work then than was done by me after joining the payroll.

Staff, it seemed, were paid on the basis of who they were—whereas the least work someone did the more they earned.

Ken said regarding the running of the camp, "It is like a charity… people just give themselves jobs; jobs are created for family and friends."

As a young man Ken had served in the British Army. He first visited Friday Bridge Camp in the mid-seventies for a fortnight's holiday—but enjoyed himself there so much that he kept returning and eventually became a staff member.

What I noticed about being a staff member in the old system was that eventually fewer people were employed to work longer, whereas in the new system more men and women were given jobs so as to do less work.

I found that as the over-employment increased, the less efficient the working standards became, in which some superior positioned individuals tended to unburden their responsibilities onto junior staff members—such as in the cookhouse where people just wanted to rush out leaving doors open and electrical equipment on after each shift.

During one morning I arrived to find one of the cooks frenetically making sandwiches... Due to a door being left open seventy packed meals had been stolen!

Due to there being no security, locals arrived unchallenged on the camp. On one weekend, at dawn, I arrived in the kitchen, to see two local men drinking lager, having spent the previous night on the camp.

One camper was injured after an intruder had attacked him in bed.

Also, men slept freely in the women's section—whereas they could have been ejected off the camp in the old system. But there was little that women in the new system could do if they didn't like sharing accommodation with other females' boyfriends, since there was no one employed to stop it!

On one evening a till from the unlocked club was stolen, consisting of several hundred pounds.

There were numerous accounts of vandalism, such as a telephone box being torn off its supporting wall, then dumped in a toilet.

The manager justified the vandalism and graffiti on huts—by saying: "When people come to the camp they see it's a shithole... so they treat it like a shithole!!"

I found the manager to be as supportive as a jelly. He was eager to let lesser employees take the blame for his errors—and was just as enthusiastic to acquire praise created from the successes of others. He had a tendency to pile work chores on employees who didn't have connections to the owner of the camp. The manager admitted to me that the well-connected staff members were underworked and drastically overpaid.

In the old days the previous labour officer organized that staff members were allowed between one and two days off a week, but in the new system only the well-connected had days off—and, there were those employees, albeit the more lowly paid, who worked for seven days a week for more than four months without a free day.

Employees were paid at different rates for doing the same work on the basis that I had equal status to John the Cowboy. I inquired why I was on a lower wage than him.

The manager retorted that we will be on the same pay, but it meant John would see his earnings decrease to my level, so consequently his wage would be lower than that made by him a year earlier.

The assistant that John and I shared was a Turk named Murat. He did the same amount of work as the Cowboy for half that John was paid.

John the Cowboy finished working as a staff member after the manager verbally attacked him for letting Murat do too much work. John said to me that he resigned, whereas the manager said that he resigned John. I decided to accept John's answer, for, since knowing him in 1980 I had found the Cowboy to be predominantly truthful.

A similar precedent happened in the catering department, where both of the cooks who had worked in the fields were on different wages. I could understand the disparity in pay if one of them had been a qualified chef—but that wasn't the case.

The higher of the two earners left his colleague to do most of the work.

The manager knew about this—and said that the highest paid cook was to be sacked on the basis that he was working for only four hours a day. The manager changed his mind—and gave him the weekend off instead. Incidentally the highest paid cook worked for two hours a day; but there again the lowest paid workers did the most amount of hours.

I conceded that it was possible people were paid more because they had spent past seasons as staff members. But this idea was abandoned after Ken saying to me that during a past season there was a meeting in which the manager stressed that no more staff were to be employed. During the same evening an Australian camper arrived at the camp. Promptly the manager gave her a job in the office. After speaking with her in the club Ken discovered that she was saving more than he was earning in a week!

Some old campers who returned to the new camp couldn't believe the slack way it was being run. These people didn't even last the week out... They complained that it had lost its character and found it hard to accept that the food was even worse than before.

Sometimes, when campers asked me the nature of their meals, I said that I didn't know, even though I had witnessed the preparation of these obscure dishes.

I found—while working in the old catering system—that the food was unhygienically handled—whose quality was poor; whereas in the new system I considered the food to be of a good standard, though there was no-one employed who could cook it properly.

My viewpoint was shared by the campers who complained about their unsatisfactory meals.

The catering department needed someone who hadn't worked on the camp during my time—a chef.

Ken said that during the past season a chef was employed who produced good meals—but he cracked up and locked himself in his room with alcohol, refusing to leave it at meal times.

John the Cowboy said regarding the chef: "He was a bit of a lesbian... His blood was mixed."

The chef was replaced by field workers.

I found that both the old and the new system needlessly lost profit.

The old labour officer often, for a variety of reasons, refused to allow new arrivals a place on the camp—even if the camp wasn't full.

In the new system campers were allowed to run up bar and accommodation bills—then later left without paying; sometimes an individual's debt totalled hundreds of pounds.

A whole week's supply of food tickets, if lost, could be bought for two pounds at the office—so that instead of paying fifty-five pounds a week in rent, campers could just pay two pounds because there was no security to make sure that people who hadn't paid were made to leave.

Due to the two pounds ticket system, some campers had double meals—and campers that went to eat later received no food because there was nothing left. Consequently complaints were made because some campers could have double meals—for an extra two pounds a week. Hence the price of a replaced set was increased to twenty pounds.

One staff member who had worked in both the old and new system, said that he wished the old labour officer was still running the camp—because it was better run by him than the new system was, which employed both a manager and labour officer.

I agreed with him—on the basis that I found the old labour officer to be more efficient, albeit ruthless, at running the camp.

One morning a camper complained to me that he couldn't find a van driver to take him at such an early time to work.

This never happened in the old system. The labour officer then was always available, making sure that the transport went out on time. These new van drivers would have been ordered from out of their beds if he had remained in charge.

In the new system there were two different sections, one of which consisted of people that started work early, while the other contained people who didn't work until later... The latter section which predominantly consisted of office workers seemed impervious to the irregularities in the other section.

There were about three times as many office workers in the new system as there were in the old one—even when there were similar amounts of campers. The new system had a computer while the old system was uncomputerized.

The owner of Friday Bridge International Camp was named Mac. Mac during the early part of the season had only spent weekends on the camp. But as the months of summer went by, Mac had been informed on the disorderly running of his camp and began to spend more weekdays on it. Once he had assessed the sheer disorder, waste and misinformation, the manager's employment was terminated.

I found Mac to be an approachable, well-intentioned, good natured person who genuinely cared about the staff and campers—but his tendency to concentrate on the good aspects of individuals' natures caused him to employ some people who were unsuitably placed in their work.

On the basis of my total of seventy-one weeks spent on the camp since 1980, I am able to conclude that key positions contained mostly unsuitable people.

Mac also found work and accommodation in various other English counties—for some campers—when a fair proportion of people on the camp were unemployed.

In the old system locals were given preferential treatment regarding entertainment and sports facilities with respect to the paying campers, whereas Mac had changed the camp to a place in which the interests of campers were placed first.

Mac, unfortunately, did receive aggravation—due to the regular visits made by the health authorities, which were unknown by me during my time as a staff member and camper in the old system. Sadly, Mac was blamed for the legacy of neglect that he had inherited from the last owners—who didn't seem to care about the mistreatment of campers. Mac, to his credit, had made plans to improve the living conditions such as the construction of better places for campers to live as well as new washroom facilities.

While working for Mac a BBC television company made a part of their documentary on East Anglian seasonal work at the camp—which I subsequently found, on watching it, to concentrate purely on the bad aspects. Its film crew wasn't interested in broadcasting the views of campers who earned more than fifty pounds a day, but only the expressions of low earners. Even though Mac had told the crew that he intended to physically improve the camp, the documentary makers ignored this and recorded the dilapidating buildings—as if the camp's new owner had no intention of improving them.

Mac also allowed campers to work for external employers.